# The Computer Professional's Guide

# The Computer Professional's Survival Guide

**Alan R. Simon**
*Simon & Associates*

**McGraw-Hill, Inc.**

New York  St. Louis  San Francisco  Auckland  Bogotá
Caracas  Lisbon  London  Madrid  Mexico  Milan
Montreal  New Delhi  Paris  San Juan  São Paulo
Singapore  Sydney  Tokyo  Toronto

Library of Congress Cataloging-in-Publication Data

Simon, Alan R.
    The computer professional's survival guide / Alan R. Simon.
        p.      cm.
    ISBN 0-07-057574-6
    1. Computers.   2. Computers—Vocational guidance.   I. Title.
QA76.25.S55      1992
004—dc20                                                    91-30183

1 2 3 4 5 6 7 8 9 0   DOC/DOC   9 7 6 5 4 3 2 1


ISBN   0-07-057574-6


*The sponsoring editor for this book was Jeanne Glasser, the editing
supervisor was Stephen M. Smith, and the production supervisor was
Pamela A. Pelton. It was set in Century Schoolbook by McGraw-Hill's
Professional Book Group composition unit.*

*Printed and bound by R. R. Donnelley & Sons Company.*

*Subscription information for BYTE Magazine:
Call 1-800-257-9402 or write Circulation Dept.,
One Phoenix Mill Lane, Peterborough, NH 03458.*

# Contents

# Preface

*The Computer Professional's Survival Guide* is the outgrowth of years of discussing career-oriented topics with colleagues in the computer profession. A number of people in the computer career field have great familiarity with their own jobs, industries, and environments—mainframe IMS maintenance programmer for a defense contractor, for example—but have little information about other computer technologies and job environments.

For many years, people could comfortably reside in niches because of the relative shortage of qualified computer programmers, analysts, hardware designers, and other professionals. The early 1990s brought an abrupt halt to these comforts for many thousands of people as recession, massive layoffs, changing technology, and other factors radically altered the employment picture in the computer profession. In these turbulent times, it is important for *every* professional in this career field to have the information contained in these pages. As the U.S. economy strengthens in the future, the topics discussed in this book will be just as important because most organizations are likely to continue to streamline their operations.

The chapters of this book include personal anecdotes and observations related to my career, which has covered a wide spectrum of job functions and specialties. My education background is in the business-oriented computer area, with undergraduate and graduate degrees in computer information systems and management information systems, respectively. I've worked as a consultant in those areas since 1982, but I have also been a systems and communications software developer for U.S. Air Force missile warning systems, a database product manager with a *Fortune* 100 computer vendor, a business development manager with a small government contractor, a university instructor and researcher, and a writer.

Many of the above positions have overlapped over the past 12 years, and through this varied career path I believe I've gained some insight into the subjects presented in this book that I wish to share. Many spirited discussions with colleagues over the years about career-related topics—jobs, technology, organizational environments, educational alternatives, and career paths—led me to write this book as a concise reference for today's and tomorrow's computer professionals.

*The Computer Professional's Survival Guide* serves not only as a stand-alone reference but as a companion to my first book, *How to Be a Successful Computer Consultant*. The topic of consulting is discussed in several places in this book, but it is not handled with the depth of the earlier book.

The main purpose of this book is to provide you with timely and relevant information to help you plan and manage your career in the computing profession. In addition, you should be able to use the information to anticipate and recognize changes in any of the areas discussed and to react to those changing situations to benefit your career.

A number of jobs and career positions are covered in Chap. 3, Computer Positions and Careers, including various software development tasks and managerial positions. The jobs discussed don't include end-user functions, such as an administrative assistant who uses a personal computer to do word processing and spreadsheet preparation tasks, or such jobs as a shipping clerk at IBM. The positions covered in that chapter and referenced throughout the book are those that are within the realm of a "computer career." In Chap. 7, Additional Career Options, some discussion of such topics as lateral moves to other career fields is presented, but only in the context of how such moves fit into your overall career strategy.

Finally, this book is intended to be your valuable reference in both highly lucrative times, such as the early and mid-1980s, and belt-tightening and economically troubled times like the early 1990s, when this book was written. I am firmly convinced, from personal experience and discussions with successful professionals in the field, that, by following the guidelines presented, you can make your computer career extremely successful regardless of the economy and other external factors.

I would like to thank each of the people who were kind enough to allow me to use their careers as profile studies. I selected the individuals—sometimes from personal knowledge, sometimes from professional reputation—to fit many of the areas discussed in this book. Without exception, each individual added far more to his profile in terms of career success tactics and strategies than had originally been anticipated. I'd like to thank the editors at McGraw-Hill for tirelessly championing this project and Ann Mergo for reviewing the manuscript and suggesting modifications. I'd also like to thank my parents, as I did in my first book, for their support throughout the years.

*Alan R. Simon*

# The Computer
# Professional's
# Survival Guide

# An Overview of the Computer Career Field

Something very important became apparent as the decade of the 1990s began: The preceding decade was completed not only in the context of chronology but also in terms of careers in the computer industry. As we will see, the computer industry is no longer the happy-go-lucky hunting ground for more and more lucrative employment opportunities; instead, it is now recognized that business cycles do indeed apply to companies and people involved in this industry.

In addition, both the profession and the employment opportunities within the industry continue to evolve. A number of factors discussed in this chapter and throughout the book—technological advances, external factors, education and training, job functions, and career paths—*must* be factored into your short- and long-term career planning.

## The Career Environment

Figure 1.1 illustrates the seven key factors that make up the computer career environment and how they relate to one another. The key point for every computer professional to recognize is that planning your career—both in the near future and over the long term—is dependent on factors in *each and every* one of the seven areas. Computer position and career choices in the past, especially during the 1980s, often consisted of frequently switching companies and jobs to realize substantial gains in salary and other forms of compensation. Career moves that proved to be mistakes could be rectified relatively easily through subsequent moves, sometimes back to former employers with compensation packages much higher than were to be had only short months before.

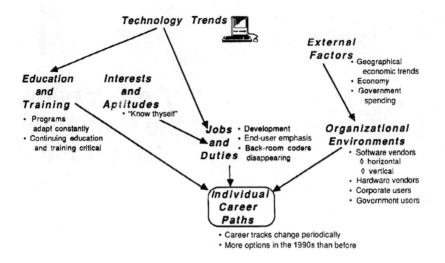

**Figure 1.1** Factors in successful computer careers.

The theme of every section of this book is that times have changed, and it is imperative to not only consider career switches more carefully than in the past but to constantly evaluate your own factors to strengthen the substance of your career.

## Technology Trends

Nearly everyone in the computer field, as well as a sizable portion of the general populace around the world, is aware that technology changes very quickly—and in an accelerating manner—in the computer industry. The computer field of the 1980s began with an overall industry environment roughly equivalent to that of the preceding decade. There were generally accepted definitions of hardware classes such as mainframes, time-sharing minicomputers, and the new personal microcomputers, along with aspects of prevalent software technology such as computer languages, user interfaces, and compilers. By the time 10 years had passed, the hardware demarcations had blurred, software technology had rapidly changed, and the commercial off-the-shelf (COTS) industry had exploded; in short, the success factors had shifted and looked nothing like they had previously.

Chapter 8 discusses computer technology trends and fast-growing areas for the 1990s. As illustrated in Fig. 1.1, the technology trends have both a direct and indirect bearing on the career of nearly every professional in the field, and they should be considered very carefully when career plans and decisions are made.

## External Factors

Though the 1980s began with a deep recession in the United States, the decade is most notable as a period of rapid and lengthy economic expansion in the United States and most of the rest of the world, resulting in burgeoning career opportunities. These opportunities occurred not only in the computer industry itself but in nearly every area of the economy that utilized computer technology.

One of the primary beneficiaries of the general and computer-specific expansion was the U.S. defense industry. The Reagan administration's massive military buildup in the United States was heavily slanted toward high technology, particularly computerized weapons and information systems. I was a U.S. Air Force officer at Space Command headquarters in Colorado Springs from 1982 until 1986, and I subsequently spent a year with a small defense contract consulting firm. At that point, a large number of major multimillion dollar systems were being procured and developed at Space Command, particularly within Cheyenne Mountain's warning headquarters, to upgrade missile warning, intelligence gathering, space surveillance, air defense capabilities, and other real-time systems. Several of these systems development efforts were in the range of hundreds of millions of dollars. Similar efforts in the Strategic Defense Initiative (SDI) program at nearby Falcon Air Force Station contributed to the local computer industry boom.

In addition, similar-scale development efforts were underway at other major U.S. Air Force commands (such as the Strategic Air Command in Omaha, Nebraska) and other U.S. military and intelligence services. The effect on employment opportunities in the computer industry in Colorado Springs and other areas was phenomenal. A new breed of Air Force computer officer developed: one who was directly involved in the procurement or development of workstation-based information systems, Ada language programming, and other state-of-the-art computer technology. Even more important to many of these officers and enlisted men and women was that their experience was directly transferable to the many local and nearby defense contractors working on and bidding for new programs, and those new jobs usually represented substantial salary increases over comparable military salaries. Retiring lieutenant colonels and colonels were collecting generous military pension payments and going to work as managers at Ford Aerospace, Martin Marietta, or other contractors. Junior computer officers separating from the service, particularly those who were proficient in the Ada programming language, often had a dozen or more job offers, many of them unsolicited. Consequently, the local economy boomed for several years.

The entire employment picture came to a grinding halt several years later. A combination of federal spending cutbacks, program delays and resulting scalebacks, contract cancellations, company sales, *and the computer industry itself,* led to an environment completely opposite from the lucrative one described above with far fewer employment opportunities, longer job searches and fewer offers than before, layoffs at both large and small firms, and drastically reduced starting salaries.

What had changed? The computer technology prevalent in the new systems hadn't. The need for newer, updated systems to replace the 1970s vintage hardware and software hadn't changed either, nor had the qualifications of the uniformed and contractor computer professionals. *Environmental factors,* similar to those that rocked California's aerospace industry in the mid-1970s through cutbacks in space programs, had overridden the other components of the employment environment shown in Fig. 1.1. The result was severe turbulence in both computer-related employment in Colorado Springs and the local economy as a whole.

Other environmental factors that have affected and will continue to affect employment in the computer industry are the economy, and more important, regional economic strengths and weaknesses. Business professionals and the general populace have long been aware of the relation between the general economy and resulting industry employment. The 1980s, however, brought about regional discrepancies in United States economic health on an arguably unprecedented scale.

In Texas, Arizona, Colorado, and other sunbelt states, the early 1980s saw great strength driven by both the energy economic sector and demographic factors. At the same time, many northeast and midwestern states saw their economic fortunes dragged down by a combination of weaknesses in manufacturing industries and farm-related woes, and earned the nickname of the "rustbelt states."

The middle years of the decade saw a nearly total reversal as real estate declines weighed heavily on many of the sunbelt states, whereas the rustbelt states, particularly those on the Atlantic seaboard, retrenched through financial services, defense spending, and computer industry growth. The strongest beneficiaries were the New England states, New York City, and the Washington, D.C., area.

The years following the 1987 stock market crash brought more reversal. New York City, New England, and most of the rest of the northeastern United States were rocked by great weaknesses in areas that had shown great strength only several years previously, such as defense spending, the computer hardware vendors, and financial services. Even California, which had shown great strength throughout most of the entire 1980s, showed stagnation and slowdowns in both the north and south for many of the same reasons as the northeastern

United States. Meanwhile, the regional economies of Texas, Colorado, and the midwest, all in serious trouble just a couple of years before, began to show signs of strength and recovery because of the energy climate, strong exports, and other factors.

It's also a safe bet that the rest of the 1990s and beyond will bring more of the same economic shifting across various regions of the United States and the rest of the world. As global economies become more intertwined than in the past, the same phased approach to economic strengths and weaknesses will be prevalent around the world as well as in the United States.

Why the economics lesson? Because of the *direct* effect on the subject of this book: employment and careers in the computer industry. We have already looked at one specific case, that of U.S. government defense spending in Colorado. Each of the economic shifts mentioned in the preceding paragraphs had strong effects on *every* individual's computer career, some in a beneficial way and others catastrophically. For example, the middle years of the 1980s brought major cutbacks in computer-related opportunities in the oil industry in the energy states (Texas, Oklahoma, and Colorado, for example) that had been booming only a little before that time, whereas computer positions in the financial services, defense, and hardware vendor areas were plentiful and lucrative. The latter years of the decade brought major cutbacks and layoffs on Wall Street—including information systems staffs—and the hardware vendors in New England, including Digital Equipment Corporation, one of the last bastions of a no-layoff tradition. As discussed previously, reverberations were also felt in the defense industry all across the United States. There was still strength, however, in such areas as Seattle and Chicago, whose economies showed some amount of resiliency.

The impacts of these external factors, including government spending and geographical economic trends, weigh heavily in the career decisions everyone in the computer profession must make, and they are explored throughout the book. Again, you must be aware of the interrelations of these factors and the other components of the computer career decision-making process, as your career and well-being will likely be directly affected.

## Job Duties and Functions

When I began my computer career in the late 1970s, there were relatively well-defined categories and job titles for most of the positions in the field. My training and background were in business-oriented applications development, and there were generally accepted definitions for such job titles as systems analysts, computer programmers, supervisors, and managers. There was a widespread belief, though obviously not totally the same in all organizations, that systems analysts would meet with users and develop system requirements and specifications, which would then be translated into functional systems and maintained by the programmers. The programmers were managed by supervisors—usually former programmers themselves—who were overseen by development managers, and so on. Similar job function breakdowns were held in the areas of system programming, hardware engineering and development, computer sales, and other career areas.

The industry today is, for the most part, much different than it was a little more than 10 years ago. Many software development career opportunities are now entitled "software engineer" (a term I intensely dislike, but that's another story), regardless of whether they are in new applications development, system programming, software maintenance, or some other area. Other positions fall under the title of "knowledge engineer," a specialist in application development who uses expert systems shells or artificial intelligence languages such as Prolog and Lisp (see Chap. 8). The various job titles and functions are discussed in further detail in Chap. 3, and the main point to remember is that, more than in the past, a job title often reveals very little about the actual functions of an employment opportunity—to say nothing of the compensation, follow-on career path, job stability, and other factors of that position.

## Organizational Environments

I mentioned in the Preface that during my career I have worked as a self-employed consultant, for a major *Fortune* 100 computer vendor, for governmental organizations at the federal and state levels, for private and public universities, and for a small startup consulting and defense contracting firm. I can unequivocally state—and the premise is discussed in further detail in Chap. 4—that the environments vary widely among these types of organizations in all areas: compensation, career growth opportunities, the type of work actually performed, numbers of hours worked and the resulting lifestyle, and in a number of other ways. Even within an overall category such as "computer vendor" there is a big distinction between developing software for a firm that is primarily a hardware company as compared with one that is a multiplatform software and services firm. These differences have *direct* bearing on the careers of everyone at those companies.

## Interests and Aptitudes

My own career in the computer industry has been somewhat business- and applications-oriented, except for a brief sojourn into the system programming and communications world while an Air Force officer. I am reasonably certain, however, that if I had tried to orient my own career toward hardware engineering, scientific programming, or mathematical modeling, I would have had *serious* problems and likely would no longer be in the computer field. In fact, I probably would have switched majors while still in college and certainly wouldn't be writing this or any other computer book. I was very fortunate that, when I was 17 and knew absolutely nothing about the computer career field, I *accidentally* chose a degree program and subsequent career path that was oriented toward my own abilities and interests. Friends of mine, however, were not so fortunate and did choose the wrong career paths for them, resulting in either delayed entry into positions more suited to their abilities or leaving the career field altogether.

Many of the subsequent chapters, when dealing with education programs, positions, and career paths, discuss how to consider your own abilities and interests in the various career-oriented decisions. This consideration is *crucial* for success in the computer profession. That is not to say, for example, that your career must exactly match your educational record and abilities and that any mismatch will automatically result in stagnation and possibly failure. I was fortunate that I was able to learn communications and system programming on the job, but can pretty much guarantee that I could not design a central processing unit or a disk controller, nor do operating system kernel programming. It is important for every computer professional—and everyone in general, regardless of his or her choice of career field—to have the insight necessary to promote career success.

## Education and Training

Chapter 6 discusses the various types of educational paths in the computer industry from computer science (and programs that operate under this title vary widely in content, as we will see) to business-oriented curricula such as computer information systems (CIS) and management information systems (MIS). The types of programs, as well as the content of each program, also evolve over time, primarily because of changes and trends in computer technology. Most educational programs at the time I was going to school (mid-1970s) were oriented toward teaching computer programming—COBOL for the CIS and MIS programs, FORTRAN for the computer science ones—and utilized key punches and card decks on mainframe systems, usually IBM or UNIVAC.

Educational curricula of all types are very different today. Many still have an emphasis on software development (expanded from just "computer programming" to encompass other steps of the development life cycle such as structured design and software testing), but more often than not utilize languages such as C, Pascal, or Ada in addition to or instead of COBOL and FORTRAN.

Personal computers, workstations, and small-end minicomputers—often run by the educational departments themselves—have replaced, or at least supplemented, computer center–operated mainframes. Fourth-generation languages (4GLs), window interfaces such as XWindows and DECWindows, and database environments have joined the traditional programming languages at many universities, and many programs feature classes in such subjects as computer law, supercomputer technology, and industry-specific subjects like computer systems in the health care industry.

What are the effects of these changes in educational programs on your career opportunities? As I mentioned, university and college programs have evolved (and will continue to change) primarily in response to changing computer hardware and software technology. Students and new professionals currently in university programs and those who have recently graduated are likely to have learned about and used 4GLs, XWindows, UNIX, and other new technologies. Although someone might have a learning curve if he or she were to accept a position as, say, Jovial maintenance on a UNISYS (Sperry) 1100/72, he or she would have strong advantages over other professionals who obtained degrees many years before and had been primarily working with "old technology" *and had not stayed current with new technologies through graduate degree programs, continuing education, and seminars.* Chapter 9 discusses various topics in the subject area of staying current, and as mentioned previously, Chap. 6 deals with various types of university and college programs and how they relate to the career successes of not only those just entering the computer profession but of those already in the field. Note also how the subject of the Career Success Profile in Chap. 2, Bill Marion, was able to remain technologically current even during the nearly 10 years he was an Air Force pilot and was officially "out of the computer industry" and was able to move into a position utilizing state-of-the-art technology without missing a beat, even in a depressed employment market.

### Career Paths

All the topics discussed in the preceding paragraphs, from technology trends to education and training, are important factors when considered individually. Considered together, however, they all directly affect the career path of every single computer professional.

That doesn't necessarily mean, for example, that if an individual's career involves the latest technology and he or she works for the "best" type of organization and the geographical and other external factors are favorable, the automatic results will be a vice presidency within 6 months and a salary in the high six figures. First, that may not even be an individual's personal goal, because many professionals in the field opt for (or because of external factors are "forced into") self-employed contract work, consulting, or teaching. Alternatively, many choose entirely untraditional career paths. There are *many* more career path options available to computer professionals today than in the past. Regardless of which path(s) you might choose—and there's no reason you can't pursue alternative options at different points in your career— all the other key factors must be considered along career journeys.

## Your Career in Context

Even though this book deals with careers in the computer profession, it is important to establish just what your specific career goals are in the larger scope of your life. Just as insight into your own strengths and weaknesses with respect to aptitude is important, so is insight into exactly what you want out of your career in comparison with the other aspects of your life.

Except in rare circumstances, a great deal of self-sacrifice is necessary to rise to the top of a corporate organization. Some people with a great deal of ability choose to make those sacrifices; others don't. There is no right or wrong answer as to your own career aspirations. The computer profession has some unique advantages in that, given its nature, you can succeed in the field even if you live in a log cabin in the back woods of West Virginia or on a sparsely inhabited island in the Pacific. You aren't likely to make it to the top of a major corporation that way, but there is nothing to prevent you from developing software, consulting, writing, or doing any of a number of other things related to the computer profession. For those who enjoy corporate, big-city life, those attributes also are available through a career in the computer field. The important thing is to try to recognize exactly the lifestyle you would like—and realize that your desires are likely to change over time—and plan your career to meet those goals.

## Summary

There are a number of factors that encompass "the computer career profession," and individual success is often predicated on the understanding and anticipation of and reaction to each of those factors. You should not only look at historical trends and the status quo in those areas—technology, external factors, organizational environments, job functions, education, interests and aptitudes, and career paths—but also vigilantly stay as current as possible in *every one* of the areas and thereby anticipate how changes in any of the factors will affect your career success.

## Career Success Profile: Charles M. Armatys, Senior Product Manager, Digital Equipment Corporation

### Educational background

B.S.E., Chemical Engineering, University of Illinois, 1975

Graduate work in chemical engineering, University of Idaho

Numerous professional development courses

### Career

Goodyear Tire and Rubber, Process Engineer, 1975–1978

Allied Chemical, Supervisor of Process Control and Instrumentation, 1978–1980

Exxon, Manager of Instrumentation Development and Control, 1980–1983

Digital Equipment Corporation, 1983–present

    Business Development Specialist, Computer Services

    Unit Manager, Consulting Services

    Product Manager, Storage Systems

    Product Manager, Database Systems

Chuck Armatys is a senior product manager in Digital Equipment's Database Systems organization. He joined Digital in 1983 after spending 8 years in the chemical industry, and his initial responsibilities were to concentrate on business development with clients in that industry. He was the product manager for Digital's HSC 50 and HSC 70 hierarchical storage controllers, producing the latter product from the initial conceptual stages. The HSC 70 was one of Digital's key product and market successes in the 1980s as a key component of DEC's VAXCluster architecture. Much of Digital's market strength has been based on VAXCluster technology, and Chuck's HSC 70 controller, which makes possible high-performance multiple paths to disks, was one of the major contributors to that success.

Following his time in the storage systems area, Chuck moved to the database field, concentrating on distributed products in the UNIX area.

**Best career move**

Moving to Digital Equipment Corporation: "My background in the chemical industry gave me the opportunity to move to DEC and concentrate on developing business in that industry."

**What he would change**

"I've never regretted any opportunity for change that I have pursued."

**Recommendations for others**

**General.** "Have a grand vision when you are talking to others about *your* career. If you have 'small aspirations'—you don't necessarily strive to reach beyond your current level of assigned tasks—keep them to yourself, particularly in a job interviewing situation. I have interviewed engineers who have stated their long-term career goals to be 'learning as many versions of UNIX as possible.' Try to have somewhat loftier goals to state.

"It is good to have a technical background, even above formal business education. Business education without practical experience in this industry is almost useless. It's better to move into a business position, such as a product manager, with a technical background.

"You should also strive to balance your life's activities. As you get into senior and upper management, you incur major commitments to your company. The rewards are there, but they should be put into perspective with other factors in your life." [Author's note: Chuck has climbed mountains on six continents, including an assault on Mt. Everest, and has a number of hobbies, including horses and photography. At various points, he has taken leaves of absence to pursue extended mountain climbs, including his time on Mt. Everest.]

**On being a successful product manager.** "Product management is not digging ditches. You must be prepared to support everything you do and every decision you make. You can't necessarily take a forecast or a business plan and expect it to stand by itself. Accountability is a key component to being a successful product manager. Organizations in which products at different stages of their life cycle are handed off to a sequence of product managers suffer from a lack of accountability. Whose responsibility is it that actual sales didn't meet forecasts...was it the original product manager who developed those forecasts and estimated returns, or the product manager who 3 years later was responsible for marketing strategy? There should, if permitted by the organizational structure, be some form of continuity.

"A product is the reflection of the product manager's personality and character. Strategy is the most creative part. This includes product positioning, how requirements are reflected in the eventual product and against those of the competition, and all other strategies and tactics. The most important thing is to know your market. If operating system XYZ is fading in terms of market share but another operating system is rising, serious consideration should be given to shifting target environments toward the rising star in system software and other technology.

"A product manager without authority over the developers can be in serious trouble. Political clout and skills, in terms of organizational politics, become crucial to negotiating your ideas. This lack of authority usually results in a weakened sense of responsibility on the part of all managers involved, since there is no one central succeed-or-fail person. This also leads to products that don't really meet market requirements, given the wide variance of meanings, for example, for 'referential integrity.' Does this include cascading deletions or not? Are all possible referential semantics included in the product? Without the product manager to be able to definitively state that 'this product will have all of these particular subfeatures,' developers may be able to skimp on the true nature of required features since their objectives are to aim for the lowest cost of development.

"Along those lines, technical knowledge and background is very important, as I already mentioned. If you as a product manager don't understand exactly what referential integrity, metadata management, and other aspects of your technology truly entail, then it is extremely difficult to gather, produce, and enforce effective product requirements.

"Creativity is also very important to a product manager. When we were doing the HSC 70, we decided that the market would support licensing the operating software in the HSC as a separate product. This brought in a substantial amount of additional revenue to Digital. Additionally, we decided to change the console terminal and printer setup from an old LA12 hardcopy terminal to a combination of a VT220 terminal and an LA50 printer. The LA12 was used only by the HSC and had an extremely high internal cost as compared with the combination package with which we replaced it. Digital saved over $7 million the first year in cost of goods sold on this alone. The only development cost was approximately 15 minutes to change a terminal driver call."

# Chapter 2

# Surviving and Thriving in Turbulent Times

**Pall of Recession Hovers over IS Staffs**

*Falling Sales, Layoffs, Job Searches Are Signs of Hard Times*

This headline from a *PC Week* article sums up the computer industry job market as the decade of the 1990s began.[1] Nearly every week since late 1987, computer professionals have opened their local newspapers, business magazines, and computer industry periodicals to read headlines announcing layoffs, voluntary severance plans, outsourcing, and other career-disrupting news. The news isn't all bad, however; the same article which featured the above headline also featured an inset box noting that "headhunters seek UNIX, C, LAN, and Database aficionados...if you worked with UNIX, if you're a C programmer, chances are people are going to be pounding your door down." [2]

In this chapter we'll examine the symptoms of a sometimes troubled employment market in the computer industry and examine how you can detect potential turbulence and how you can take steps to mitigate the disruption to your career and personal life. We'll also see, in the Career Success Profile at the end of the chapter, how one particular individual was able to reenter the computer field after a 10-year absence without missing a beat and the steps he took to ensure that, even though he was an Air Force pilot during that time, he stayed up to date with hardware, software, and particularly communications technology.

## Fifty Ways to Leave a Job

Well, maybe not fifty, but let's look at the major influences on computer career disruption.

## Downsizing

Downsizing has become a polite term for the dreaded L word: layoffs. However, downsizing encompasses more than just involuntary termination from someone's job; it also includes the many variations of early retirement and voluntary severance plans. Major computer vendors, particularly IBM and Digital Equipment Corporation, began several types of voluntary severance and early retirement plans in the late 1980s, many of them accompanying the closure of specific manufacturing plants. Those two companies in particular have had long traditions of avoiding involuntary layoffs at all costs, and (according to business and trade periodical speculation at the time) wished to keep their traditions intact. As the economy as a whole, and corporate earnings in particular, worsened, Digital Equipment announced its first ever "involuntary severance program" in early 1991 for an estimated 3500 people, with the terminations to take place over the first 6 months of that year. To many, that was an indication that the problems in the computer industry were far more serious than during past slumps.

Digital was not alone in facing that unpleasant decision. Hardware and software vendors across the United States and around the world saw eroding revenues and profits, increasing losses, and other indications that rapid staff buildups during the preceding several years were burdening their firms with cumbersome and weighty overhead in ever-worsening times. Also, the problems were not confined solely to vendors, because user organizations large and small saw their data processing and information systems organizations consuming too large a portion of their resources in troubled times. Consulting organizations, service organizations, and nearly every other type of company associated with the computer industry also were affected.

There were and are, however, success stories to be found among the many firms in the industry. Firms that fill particular niche markets and provide services that were being cut from larger companies found an ever-increasing business base and corresponding revenues and profits.

Downsizing actions—we'll just call them staff cuts—have taken various forms. Some have been of the traditional "Here's two weeks' pay and clean out your desk by 5:00" form; others have included very generous financial packages. Some of the earlier IBM voluntary severance plans that accompanied plant closures provided 2 years of salary plus an additional $25,000 to each person who didn't wish to move to a new position elsewhere in the corporation, and the early Digital plans provided a sliding financial scale based on the number of years the employee had been with the firm. Although no financial settlement is apt to be comforting to someone who has just lost his or her job, the person who receives enough to provide a financial bridge until further employment is found or a business is started has at least some cushion to what is undoubtedly a stressful time for most.

## Outsourcing

One of the factors that has led to some of the staff cuts we have just discussed is the rise in "outsourcing," which is the computer industry's version of "life is a circle." Back in the early, mainframe-intensive days of computing, many organizations couldn't afford their own computers and the associated operational and development staff and contracted with service bureaus to provide their data processing. The growth of minicomputers, followed by personal computers and ever-more-affordable technology, brought the ownership of computing facilities into the realm of any organization that could afford $500 for a PC. Starting in the late 1980s, however, a strange (to me, at least) phenomenon began to occur, as major corporations began "outsourcing" their corporate information systems functions to vendors and service bureaus. These corporations made the conscious decision that it was more cost-effective, because of the continuing rapid changes in technology, to utilize the services of third parties rather than run their own operations in-house.

The inevitable consequence of the growth of outsourcing was that most of the information system staffs of the organizations that divested themselves of their data processing departments were no longer needed. Many of the displaced personnel simply moved to the firm that acquired the outsourcing contract, but others either chose not to join the new company or were in overhead-intensive positions that weren't needed by the outsourcing vendor.

Outsourcing appears to be affecting IBM mainframe-based organizations particularly hard and Digital-based companies also. Over 30 percent of companies with IBM mainframes surveyed in late 1990 and early 1991 were actively pursuing or considering outsourcing, and 20 percent of Digital-based organizations were thinking the same way.[3]

## Mergers and acquisitions

Even though the merger and acquisition (M&A) fever of the last half of the 1980s has cooled because of pressures in the financial community, the effects of M&As and resulting restructurings have had their impact on computer professionals. Even allowing for adjustment and integration periods, the inevitable result of most M&As was redundancy in the IS staff or, in the case of divestitures to pay down some of the takeover debt, sudden losses of corporate information-processing assets as divisions and companies were sold. Either way, the M&A climate has had long-lasting effects on corporate IS staffs and the careers of those affected.

## User industry slumps

As was mentioned earlier, it hasn't been just the slumping fortunes of hardware and software vendors that has disrupted the careers of many in the computer industry. User industries also have seen dramatic slowdowns in recent years. In Chap. 1 we discussed the financial and defense industries' rising and falling fortunes and the resulting effects on geographical economies and the careers of many of those involved in those industries. A nearly infallible rule is that when the line functions of an organization suffer because of industry slowdowns, the staff functions—in this case, computer and information systems—will also, and so will the personnel assigned to those positions.

## Technology shifts

Chapter 1 discussed how shifts in hardware, software, and communications technology affect the career potentials of everyone involved in the computer industry. More specifically, those who are experienced in "new" (or newly appreciated) technologies—witness the quotation at the beginning of this chapter and its reference to C and UNIX skills—are more likely to survive staff reductions than those whose technical skills are years behind the times. Even if affected by cuts, the people skilled in sought-after technologies are far more likely to find new positions *quickly* than those whose most recent software development experience is in antiquated languages on obsolete hardware.

## How to Prepare for Career Uprooting

The first thing *every single reader* should realize is that times are changing in the computer industry and *no one* is 100 percent safe from one or more of the career disruptions discussed in the preceding section. When even companies with years-old no-layoff traditions find themselves having to make painful cuts of long- as well as short-term employees, no one should become too complacent in his or her current job environment. That is also true of people who have their own firms, most typically consulting or custom software development companies. Although some organizations do choose to eliminate in-house staff in favor of outside, temporary resources, others try to pare outside expenditures as much as possible before cutting into their own personnel.

Look for early signs of trends. Learn to recognize danger signs in user industries, the computer industry as a whole, and specific segments. Stories headlined like the one cited at the beginning of this chapter usually detail where current and projected weaknesses may lie. If, for example, you work for a database vendor and begin reading articles in computer and business periodicals about flat growth in the database software, you can consider that an early warning indicator. It doesn't necessarily mean that you will be facing a layoff the next week, but it does mean that unless conditions improve—and you should look for those indications as well—there may be fallout that will affect your position and possibly your career path.

The same is true of user industries. If you work in the defense sector and read story after story about pressures to dramatically reduce defense spending and increase program cancellations, it may be time to consider a shift in industry specialization to prevent sudden unemployment. That is discussed further in Chap. 5 in respect to career planning.

## Defensive Actions

There are a number of steps you can take to either minimize or help to eliminate the threat to your personal job security and career. One of the first things you can do is make sure that you are as familiar as possible with the latest in computer technology, *whether or not your current job utilizes it*. Chapter 8 discusses some of the most promising areas of specialization over the next decade within the computer industry, and Chap. 9 contains key steps to staying abreast of technological advances. Look at problem areas in your organization—development productivity, software maintenance costs, network inefficiencies, and others—and learn how object-oriented languages and databases, CASE tools, client-server computing, and other technologies that are not in use in your organization can solve real-life problems and reduce costs, improve productivity, or whatever your firm's most pressing problem is.

*Become the expert*—and make it widely known that you *are* an expert—on those new technologies. In the event your organization must make staff reductions, you may gain a bit of an edge in keeping your position because of your now widely known expertise. There are, of course, other factors involved in staff reductions than just technical ability; examples are political clout, relative salaries, and age. However, every little bit helps. And, as was mentioned before, if you do wind up being terminated, your chances in an ever-tightening job market to acquire a new position elsewhere will be greatly enhanced by not only your technical abilities but also your demonstrated drive to stay up to date with new advances.

Another defensive action is to pursue at least a semiactive job search. If rumors begin to circulate about layoffs at your company, you should make sure that your résumé is updated, "just in case." You may want to make a casual inquiry with an executive-recruiting firm about open positions at their clients for which you might be qualified. When a computer industry job fair comes to town, you might want to take the afternoon off from work and attend. *Don't feel guilty about exploring new career possibilities*; although I am all in favor of giving a 100 percent effort for your company, you also need to consider your personal needs and those of your family, if applicable. If you suddenly find yourself without a job and with a minimal severance package, a delayed job search that was due to company loyalty may prove to be costly.

While we're discussing the personal side of this turbulent employment picture, there are a number of things you should do if warning signs do appear. Try your best to build your personal savings to provide a cushion against sudden unemployment. Scale down your personal debt and postpone unnecessary major purchases; in short, follow the many guidelines presented in personal finance periodicals and in the many articles that appear in your local newspaper. Financial health, planning, and fiscal responsibility should be personal goals in any case, but particularly in a time of unpredictable industry employment outlook, you should try to reduce or eliminate as many problem areas as possible so you can concentrate on your career stability and, if necessary, job searches.

Another step you may wish to consider is moonlighting: pursuing outside activities in addition to your full-time employment. You might do some contract programming work for or provide consulting services to small local businesses in the evenings and on weekends. You might write articles or books on topics on which you have a great deal of expertise. Moonlighting provides three major benefits. First, it gives you an opportunity to learn new technologies in addition to trying to integrate them into your job. When I entered active duty in the U.S. Air Force in 1982, I was assigned to be a software developer for one of the nation's missile warning defense systems. Much to my distress, I arrived in Colorado Springs to find that I would be programming in Jovial on a Sperry Univac 1100/42 computer; a seldom-used programming language on antiquated hardware. I had already developed software on an 1100/42 during a college programming job, and I was looking at 4 years of little practical experience for my postmilitary civilian career. That was when I began my consulting activities, not so much for the additional income as to avoid becoming technologically obsolete.

The second benefit of moonlighting, obviously, is the additional income. Whether you earn enough to buy a new car or just enough to take a weekend vacation, additional income is always welcomed by most people.

Third, moonlighting can provide exposure to career opportunities that you otherwise might not find. A consulting client might become a future employer, as could a software vendor whose database or user interface product you use in your outside work.

No outside activities should involve conflict of interest with your primary job. When I began consulting, I was unable to pursue any defense-related work because of my primary position as an Air Force software development officer. In my case, violation of those conflict-of-interest regulations could have resulted in penalties up to and including a dishonorable discharge and imprisonment. In most cases, conducting outside activities that are detrimental to your primary employer will result, at best, in a derailed career path at that company and at worst in being fired. You should be aware of any organizational or corporate policies affecting outside activities and use your own judgment as to the course of action to take. Legal and ethical considerations aside, outside activities are a good defensive, preventative course to consider in an uncertain job climate.

You should also give extra-careful consideration to job changes in tough times. Computer professionals have been notorious job hoppers, moving from one position to another at different firms in an almost mercenary manner. Given the environment which we are discussing in this chapter, job changes should be for a good reason rather than "Oh well, it's time for a change." Job searches are likely to take longer than in even the recent past, so extra caution should be taken before accepting a new position. Such unforeseen problems as conflicts with supervisors aren't likely to be remedied by another quick job change.[4]

## Options

Let's assume that, despite taking one or all of the defensive actions discussed in the previous section, you suddenly find yourself "downsized" and without a job. What are some of the options that you now have?

The first, and probably most obvious, is to try to seek a similar position at another company. Chapter 9 discusses some of the many courses of action to take with respect to a job search. In some cases, however, you don't wish or are unable to acquire a position with another firm. You might look at solo work, turning your outside contract software development or consulting work into a full-time job. Many people who are suddenly laid off in the computer industry find ready-made consulting clients in their former employers. Logic would seem to dictate that if you find yourself without a position, your position was either redundant or obsolete at your company. In reality, though, layoffs seldom follow reason. High-level corporate directives to eliminate, say, 2000 positions often get translated into terminating 2000 lower-level employees, some of whom are performing critical tasks. Many of those functions still need to be carried out, and managers often turn to their suddenly former employees to, in effect, continue in exactly the same jobs but now in a contract capacity. It may sound rather inefficient, but believe me, it often happens in exactly that way. Contract work doesn't have to be a permanent career option; instead it may be a bridge until something permanent comes along. You should, however, specify in any contract for temporary work that you reserve a specific amount of time for searching for permanent employment or for other temporary work.[5] You want to avoid completing a temporary contract without any follow-on prospects.

Since job searches are likely to take longer than in the past, sudden unemployment may be designated on your résumé by a gap of several months or longer. Contract or consulting work can fill this time gap, but in the absence of those activities your résumé will passively note your unemployment for years to come. In the past, too much of a gap between positions was often a career kiss of death, since employers felt (often unfairly) that there must be something wrong with your skills if you couldn't find a job for 6 months. In these widely realized tough times in the computer industry, however, employers tend to be a bit more understanding, especially if you helped fill the gap with temporary activities.[6]

Others may decide to move into new careers, sometimes in the computer industry and other times outside it. A software developer laid off from an aerospace company might take a software sales position at a database software vendor, and a business development manager terminated by a hardware vendor might take a noncomputer position at a manufacturing firm. Someone tired of corporate life may choose to get a doctoral degree and become a tenure-track instructor in a computer science department at a local university. Some geographical areas may have tough job markets at various times, based on economic climates and other factors (recall the examples cited in Chap. 1), and that may hinder career switching or even basic job searches.

For those who are relatively financially secure, sudden unemployment may be an opportune period to take off from full-time work and pursue other interests (as long as the money lasts). Extended travel, volunteer work, writing a novel, and other activities unrelated to the computer profession may be an excellent refresher for someone who is burned out and disillusioned, and they can lead to great personal satisfaction. As an aside, you don't have to wait until you are involuntarily laid off to pursue outside, noncomputer activities, as evidenced by the career success profile in Chap. 1. Paid and unpaid sabbaticals are an excellent way to achieve a similar balance between professional and personal activities.

## Summary

There is no denying that the times in which this book is being written and published are trying ones for many involved in the computer industry. As with the areas discussed in Chap. 1, the key to survival and success in unpredictable times is to take a proactive approach to the problem rather than just sit by helplessly while waiting for events to take their toll on you, your career, and your life. Times may get better as economic conditions improve and new technologies are introduced and accepted. In the meantime, you owe it to yourself to carefully and objectively analyze your own career situation with respect to the factors discussed in this chapter and take whatever defensive and preventative steps are necessary to either protect your current job or position yourself to move as seamlessly as possible into the next step in your career path.

### Career Success Profile: William Marion, Information Center Analyst, San Mateo County Information Services Department

#### Educational background

B.S., Computer Information Systems, Arizona State University, 1980

M.B.A., City University, Bellevue, Washington, 1989

#### Career

Programming Instructor, Arizona Technical School, 1979–1980

Computer Systems Development Officer, U.S. Air Force, 1980–1981

U.S. Air Force Pilot, 1981–1990

Information Center Analyst, San Mateo County Information Services Department, 1990–present

Adjunct Professor/Instructor, Golden Gate University, 1990–present

In the course of conducting research for this book, I queried several hiring managers and recruiters about the following situation:

"Assume someone has been 'out of the computer industry' for the past 10 years while flying airplanes. What would the chances be for him to 'rejoin' the profession and obtain a midlevel position using state-of-the-art computer technology on a daily basis?"

Every single person responded with answers along the lines of "not a chance," "maybe an entry-level position and at an extraordinarily low salary," or "not in this economy; maybe next year." For those of you who are facing difficult job searches or who fear that you are locked into dead-end technology, I would recommend paying careful attention to this particular Career Success Profile, because the lessons presented may be extremely critical to your career success.

Bill Marion spent a year as an Air Force computer systems officer in the early 1980s developing mainframe-based simulations systems. He then applied to and was accepted for pilot training and spent the next 8 years (after a year of pilot training) flying C-130 and C-5 cargo transport planes, including a 2-year stint on the island of Guam. For purposes of this book, it's not his flying during those years that is important, but rather how he turned his "additional duties" over that period into a continuous sequence of state-of-the-art computer work that gave him the opportunity to reenter the computer industry without a hitch after he left active duty.

Bill's first assignment following pilot training was at Keesler Air Force Base in Biloxi, Mississippi. At the time, personal computers were just beginning to make their way into Air Force flying units but few people knew anything about the systems, and the hardware and software mostly sat unused. Bill developed Basic and dBASE logistics programs to track personal flying equipment—gloves, flight jackets, parachutes—that replaced a paper-intensive, manual system. He developed several iterations of this system, moving from a batch-reporting system to a query-processing, database-based set of applications. At the same time, he also supported mainframe Cobol applications for wartime mobility processing. Both efforts were in addition to his primary flying duties with the famed Hurricane Hunters squadron.

When he was transferred to the island of Guam, Bill repeated his efforts from his prior assignment, adding PC-based applications for mobility and aircrew recall management. He also developed a microcomputer-based flight planning system that offloaded work from and supplemented a mainframe-based system back in the continental United States. As a consequence of Bill's work in the flight-planning area, his unit was able to significantly improve flight plan turnaround and save the Air Force substantial financial resources. Again, these development efforts were carried out along with his primary flying duties, this time with the Typhoon Chasers squadron.

About this time, Bill was considering leaving active duty and returning to full-time computer work. His activities over the past several years had kept him up to date with many aspects of computer technology, more, ironically, than if he had remained at his initial assignment developing mainframe-based simulations. He began work on an M.B.A. degree, selecting a program that not only had an emphasis on information systems but featured courses on local area networks and other practical applications of computer and communications technology.

His big break came when he was reassigned to fly C-5 cargo transports at Travis Air Force Base near Sacramento, California. He arrived to find a unit that was, in the words of one squadron commander, "flying $200 million, state-of-the-art planes and doing flight planning on the back of pizza boxes." The squadrons would literally take cardboard pizza boxes—new ones, not used, greasy ones—and draw grid-based flight plans with a planning horizon of only 1 month. The system was rife with problems, including training (some missions fulfilled training requirements, but that wasn't reflected on the pizza box wall chart and many aircrews found themselves scheduled for unnecessary training while others who needed the training faced long delays) and configuration control of the pizza box system among the different desks that had input to the flight system. There were also interface requirements with a Sperry mainframe and several systems that resided there that required manual input of flight data.

The organization had five microcomputers but, as at Keesler AFB several years before, they were sitting there unused. Bill developed a prototype flight-planning system by using the database component of an integrated software package. He identified problems with the initial prototype, most notably in the requirements for multiple data entry and reporting facilities. With the knowledge obtained from his LAN master's degree course, he implemented a five-node Ethernet LAN by using 1-Mbit/s twisted-pair wire. Bill and several other unit members installed the hardware and network software, as well as Bill's applications software, by themselves. They also put an administrative management system for performance appraisals and other functions onto the LAN and developed a scheduling system.

Bill's work gained the attention of senior generals at Military Airlift Command (MAC), the parent command for his flying unit. Following a conference at Scott Air Force Base (MAC headquarters) near St. Louis, he was given a set of additional requirements to implement into his system over the next 6 weeks. His work was then merged with a window-based, mouse-driven system developed at another Air Force base for the purpose of providing a standard, PC-LAN–based system for all MAC bases and units.

Again, during this 2-year period, nearly all of this work (except for the dedicated, 6-week period described in the preceding paragraph) was done along with Bill's flying responsibilities. The systems also became proof-of-concept work for several aerospace and computer industry vendors who were attempting to get involved in flight-planning applications.

When it came time to leave active duty, Bill easily obtained a teaching position at Golden Gate University along with a *midlevel* position with San Mateo County in California, where today he works with client-server technology, office automation, local area networks, systems integration (personal computers, AS/400 midrange systems, and IBM mainframes), graphical user interfaces (GUIs), C programming, and project planning, among other technologies and managerial disciplines. Not bad for someone who, according to "the experts," would have to start over from scratch just as if he were a new graduate.

What were the secrets of Bill's success?

1. He recognized the need—which turned out to be critical—of staying up-to-date with advances in computer hardware and software, even while he was flying.
2. He *acted* on that need: He implemented successful, real-life applications during every single assignment he had, building an uninterrupted string of progressive, results-oriented, and increasingly technically sophisticated accomplishments.
3. He started and completed a master's degree that emphasized practical, useful technologies which he was able to incorporate into his past and present work.
4. He *planned* his career and developed a strategy (see Chap. 5) which supported his goal of reentering employment in the computer industry. And, once again, he *acted* on that strategy.

### Best career move

"Doing all the computer work and learning what the up-and-coming technologies were. I knew I couldn't rely on what I had learned in school 10 years ago to help me get a job."

### What he would change

"I would have liked to have been able to get my master's degree while going to school full-time, but the way I did it was the best practical way at the time."

### Long-term career objective

"To work as a consultant with state-of-the-art technologies."

### Recommendations for others

**General.** "I never was sure if I was going to stay on active duty past my flying commitment, and really didn't want to fly commercially. With all the low-end systems suddenly available, I was able to continue working with and learning about computer hardware and software even though officially I was a pilot.

"I kept reading—and still do—stacks of trade journals to see what trends were emerging.

"I also needed a master's degree that I could begin while stationed in Guam and continue once I returned to the mainland. The program I picked allowed me to do that, and it was the best of the several I investigated as far as having practical courses in LANs and other subjects. It might not have the glamour of a degree from M.I.T., but it served me well in teaching me new technologies and helping me get back into full-time work. I also didn't relearn the same things I had learned as an undergraduate, such as batch COBOL programming, even though both were information systems–oriented programs."

**On job searches.** "Once I knew I was getting out of the Air Force, I began looking at the classified and display advertisements [for employment]. This was about 7 or 8 months before I was actually on terminal leave. I saw that LANs were popular and oriented my résumé—and my search—toward my LAN and PC experience.

"I went to job fairs, looking at who was hiring and in what areas. For family reasons, I needed to remain roughly in the same geographic area—northern California—and was a bit concerned because the slowdown here was just beginning.

"I had originally been considering just teaching, and had tailored my résumé toward that experience, since I taught courses while I was in college and had already obtained my California teaching credentials. Once I realized that I had a good chance at using my LAN and PC experience to get a job in that area, I revised my résumé to emphasize the practical experience with these technologies.

"At the last job fair I attended, I had 12 to 15 screening interviews and was offered the job at San Mateo County. There were others—particularly defense contractors, who were interested in my doing simulation work similar to what I had done 10 years ago—but the position at the county looked like a good opportunity to extend my LAN and small systems work. It has turned out well, since I've gotten involved in office information systems, especially electronic mail, and client-server systems."

## End Notes

1. *PC Week*, Dec. 24/31, 1990, p. 92.
2. Ibid.
3. "IBM users get outsource itch," *Computerworld*, Mar. 4, 1991, p. 1.
4. "Job hoppers lose their bounce," *Computerworld*, Jan. 7, 1991, p. 78.
5. "Temporary work can soothe layoff sting," *Computerworld*, Jan. 21, 1991, p. 1.
6. "Success story: Hunting for a skills niche," *Computerworld*, Jan. 28, 1991, p. 74.

# 3

# Computer Positions and Careers

This chapter will provide a comprehensive discussion of the job functions you might pursue during your career in the computer profession. No doubt you are aware of many of the jobs discussed here, particularly if you have been in the field for some time. Nearly everyone, however, should find some value in reviewing job functions with which he or she might not be familiar. If, as was highly recommended earlier in this book, you are looking at your career and planning your progression, the information in this chapter will be of immense value to you. That holds true if you are contemplating job changes.

Every effort is made, when discussing the many job functions, to provide you with the near- and long-term outlook for positions in those areas. Keep in mind, though, as technology, the economy, and the other factors explored in Chap. 1 change over time, you should always try to obtain as up-to-date information as possible.

In addition, salary ranges are not provided for these positions for several reasons. First, salaries vary widely over time, as well as by user industry and geographical location. For example, a chief information officer (CIO) or vice president of information systems in the banking industry was likely to receive an average salary of $10,000 *less* in 1990 than in 1989.[1] The best way to explore current salary ranges is to request the periodic salary surveys published by Source EDP, Robert Half, and other recruiting organizations. These salary surveys contain breakdowns by region, user industry, and job position, as well as other useful career-oriented information.

Figure 3.1 illustrates the computer position family we will look at in this chapter.

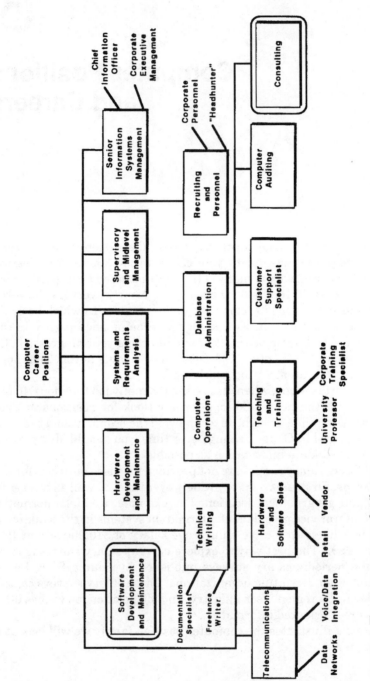

**Figure 3.1**  The computer career family tree.

## Software Development Professionals

If this book had been written 10 years ago, this section would likely have been titled "Computer Programmer." In the past decade, the distinctions between systems analysts, programmer/analysts, and "plain old programmers" have blurred, leading to the need for a general category by the above title.

In addition, the software development field has so many characteristics that it is impossible to include a list with clear demarcations among the different development specializations. Instead, you might look at the software development area as a three-dimensional matrix, as shown in Fig. 3.2.

Every software development position has elements of each axis of the matrix. For example, a particular job might involve maintenance software that utilizes graphical interfaces extensively. Of course, many positions also overlap boundaries on one or more axes, involving, for example, a combination of new development and maintenance for database and CASE applications.

The following paragraphs discuss the various characteristics of software development from a number of aspects. Again, keep in mind the matrixed relations among these characteristics and how the characteristics relate to one another in various career positions. The material discussed is not intended to provide a how-to guide for software development, design, programming, or any other technical topic. Instead, it shows the software development area in the light of the career-oriented topics discussed throughout this book.

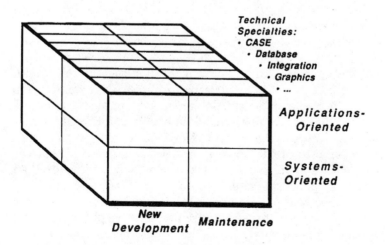

**Figure 3.2**   The software development matrix.

## Applications development

A majority of development positions have an emphasis on designing, coding, testing, and delivering applications software. Whether applications are vertical—industry-specific, such as real estate office management—or horizontal—crossing industry boundaries, such as word processing—all these programs are *user-oriented* as opposed to *system-oriented* (which are discussed in the next section).

Many computer science graduates, and most business-oriented information systems graduates, begin their careers in an applications development area. In the past, applications programmers typically took specifications from systems analysts and developed system designs; those designs were then coded in a programming language by the same or other programmers. Gradually, programmer/analyst positions grew at organizations that realized the value of having the developers work directly with the users of the systems. Today, especially in belt-tightening times, most organizations have staffs of programmer/analysts with job titles such as "software engineer," "software consultant," or sometimes still "programmer/analyst," all of whom are responsible for multiple stages of the software development lifecycle.

Most readers have had applications programming positions in the past or might be doing such work at present and are familiar with the job tasks involved. The way in which positions today often differ from those of 10 or 20 years ago is the technology involved and the adherence to well-defined lifecycles and standards. Progressive organizations extensively use computer-aided software engineering (CASE) tools for all areas of the development lifecycle from requirements collection to testing and maintenance, along with prototyping facilities and a wide range of productivity enhancers such as graphical platforms for user interfaces and databases for storage management. Even those in applications maintenance positions with few or no new development responsibilities often have a variety of tools to assist them in their work. In addition, the desire of organizations to improve the quality and turnaround of their applications maintenance work has led to the adoption of many standards from relational databases and SQL interfaces to enterprise architectures such as SAA or NAS. There is still a "software first" mentality in the application development world, but the meaning of "software" in this context has come to include more than just choosing an operating system, database platform, or commercial package to fit the given requirements. Instead, it has come to include graphical user interfaces, the enterprise architecture platforms, tools and utilities, client and server components, and many other aspects that weren't applicable in the past. A highly qualified, successful applications developer must be aware of those many aspects, for even if they aren't currently among his or her job tasks, they will soon be.

### Systems software development

One of the outside reviewers of this book's proposal and outline commented that there really wasn't much need for systems programmers anymore, and that area of specialization was an extremely poor one for an entry-level person to choose. I can personally tell you that not only is the comment incorrect but, in the words of a Denver recruiting firm office manager, "Applications programmers are a dime a dozen. Systems programmers—those with skills in capacity planning and other systems-oriented areas—are in great demand by our client companies."

It is true that in some cases, the move toward standardization in operating systems, peripheral device interfaces, and architectures has somewhat impacted the need for systems programmers at some vendors, since each and every company no longer needs to have its own proprietary operating system, compilers, disk and tape drivers, and other unique systems software. I also agree that the trend in the past has been for most systems programmers to be divorced from customers and other users and to concentrate instead on squeezing out those couple of extra micro-whatevers of performance.

At this very moment, however, there are tens of thousands of systems programmers employed at vendors ranging from giants such as AT&T, IBM, and Microsoft to startup software firms to research organizations. These people are developing new research operating systems, maintaining variants and new versions of existing operating systems, developing database management systems and CASE tools, porting compilers to new operating systems, layering system management utilities with graphical interfaces, and carrying out hundreds of other tasks. Systems programmers at user organizations manage software and hardware capacity and assist with the planning cycles for new information systems by evaluating operating systems, database products, and other system software.

The point is that systems programming is far from dead as a specialty. Many very brilliant computer professionals who don't wish to deal with end users or develop industry-specific applications opt for careers in systems software development rather than the applications area. Career options do tend to be somewhat more limited, because most user organizations don't have operating system or compiler developers and system software specialists therefore tend to cluster toward employment at vendors. However, the trend toward standardization discussed above gives someone a bit more latitude in moving among vendors. A Honeywell GCOS operating system developer had a bit of a learning curve if he or she wished to move to Sperry Univac to be an Exec 8 programmer. However, a UNIX or MS-DOS utilities developer at any given vendor could easily jump to a new position with a new company and, for the most part, be productive immediately.

### Software maintenance and modification

Software maintenance is often viewed as a necessary evil. Most developers don't want anything to do with the function, but someone has to do it, and new graduates often cut their teeth fixing bugs and making enhancements and modifications of existing applications or systems programs.

Maintenance programming follows much the same characteristics and other criteria discussed in this section. The development lifecycle still applies, since modification requirements must be collected, specifications and design documents must be produced, and code must be written. The primary differences are the obvious constraints of existing applications and systems most currently in use by real-life users. They complicate the actual implementation of maintenance code versions, since existing data must keep its integrity and downtime often must be minimized. Therefore, maintenance software development professionals often are required to plan installations and other user-impact areas with a great deal more care than if a brand-new implementation were occurring. Those planning skills are critical to anyone involved in software maintenance.

### Software development niches

The topics and aspects of software development that we've discussed so far are somewhat general in nature, since they apply to a multitude of development areas. There are, however, a number of highly specialized niches for those who wish to move out of the mainstream of software development into more refined areas. An advantage of this type of software development career is somewhat higher compensation than received by the average developer, which is earned by the higher skill levels required by the various tasks of these positions. A disadvantage might be less flexibility in career options, given the highly specialized nature of these types of jobs. However, adherence to the many lessons and examples presented in this book will prevent someone from getting locked into a particular niche in the event the technology, climate, and other factors change. Moves into other areas shouldn't be a problem. Three of the many specialized areas are:

1. *Graphics.* In this context, graphics means more than just working with graphical user interfaces and developing graphics drivers. Instead, it means doing *extensive* work in computer animation, imaging, and related areas. Many movies today use computer-generated animation heavily, and developers with strong aptitudes for graphics might consider a career working for a firm that does motion picture computer animation. In fact, I once heard an Air Force general puzzle over why the graphical displays and holograms used in movies looked so much better than the military's real-life systems and wonder if it were possible to get Disney Studios, instead of the "regular" defense contractors, to develop warning systems for the Air Force.

2. *Communications and networks.* Most software developers will eventually work with communications capabilities as applications become more and more distributed and networks play an ever-increasing role in the resulting systems. Just as with graphics, however, you can go beyond the periphery and become a "true" communications specialist. Then your job is not to interface with communications and network facilities, but to actually write the protocol drivers, device interfaces, gateway and bridge software, and other components of computer communication.

3. *Embedded systems.* Much of the embedded system work to date has been in the civilian and military sectors of the aerospace industry, along with other areas of weaponry. Space systems, missiles, and other offensive and defensive weapons often have specialized embedded computer systems. Despite the projected slowdowns in military spending, embedded systems are finding their way into other applications such as "smart homes" (computer-controlled home environments), automobile components, and other aspects of everyday life. Embedded systems typically don't have operating systems, compilers, and utilities, and in fact they aren't even the development platform for the software; the code is usually written elsewhere and downloaded into the embedded system. Those who work with embedded systems must be extensively aware of error processing and recovery, since it's a bit difficult to read a dump and fix a bug on a satellite many miles above the earth. The special techniques that support software in those environments are different from those of a typical inventory application.

### Skills for success

Regardless of the areas of software development in which you might choose to concentrate your efforts, each area involves a similar set of skills. Every good software developer, even a systems programmer, with career aspirations beyond coding, works with users. The users for those involved with applications are fairly obvious. Systems programmers have as their users the applications developers and anyone else who uses a graphical or command line interface to a utility or operating system. The most successful software developers are those who can communicate with those users, and particularly those who can translate true needs into system requirements: the same skills that are required of a highly qualified systems analyst.

Coding skills are obviously an important part of software development. Abilities with multiple third- and fourth-generation languages, as well as database platforms, user interfaces, run-time libraries, and the other mechanisms mentioned earlier, are important parts of a coder's repertoire.

Creativity also is very important. Often, a particular task or problem can't be solved in an obvious manner; a bit of creativity is required to get around limitations of languages or systems. For example, Ashton-Tate's dBASE III didn't support arrays, which were sorely needed in a system I was building several years ago. Fortunately, I came across a dBASE programming tip in a magazine on how to simulate arrays by using the STR function. While I had been totally baffled by the problem, some creative programmer whose tips had been published in that magazine solved my problem for me in a way that I hadn't even considered.

Finally, staying current (see Chap. 9) on programming languages and the other technologies discussed here is very important. Given the rapidity with which technology is changing, as discussed throughout this book, you can't afford to be unaware of, for example, object-oriented languages and databases, graphical query languages, and other technologies which aren't even thought of today. Although you may not use them immediately, they may be an important part of your career progression.

### Educational background

Depending on what you wish to do in the software development field, different educational backgrounds can serve different needs. If you wish to concentrate on systems programming, a computer science degree with courses in operating systems, compilers, language theory, and other system-oriented subjects is important. That is not to say that educational background is absolutely essential to work in the area, since I mentioned earlier that my early days in the U.S. Air Force were spent doing systems and communications software development, despite business-oriented training. My computer science educational background came in the form of on-the-job training, continuing education, and system-specific training courses and a lot of assistance from senior coworkers. Regardless, courses in structured analysis and design, structured programming, and similar topics, whether taken in an undergraduate, graduate, or postgraduate manner, lend a great deal of assistance to even the most talented developer's work.

Applications developers have wide variations in their educational backgrounds from computer science to information systems to, possibly, a noncomputer college degree. The important thing for applications developers to remember with respect to educational background is that there is a great likelihood of not having an exact match between courses taken in college and real-life job responsibilities, and the blanks should be filled in through the same combination of continuing education, on-the-job training, and mentoring (see Chap. 9) that I discussed earlier as helping my own career.

### Career progression

The traditional, "standard" career path for software developers has been to progress to a supervisory or entry-level position, then on to a midlevel management job, and then, for some, to a senior management role in a corporation or large organization. There are a number of factors which should cause anyone to carefully consider his or her options with respect to this career path, and they are discussed in more detail in Chap. 5. Briefly, the glut of development supervisors and managers at major organizations, coupled with the various environmental factors discussed in the first chapter, means that there is less opportunity for the multitudes of today's developers to follow that particular career journey. Therefore, you should carefully analyze your own organization's environment and structure and plan your career accordingly. Use that information together with the various aspects of insight discussed throughout this book. There are many career options discussed in this chapter; a broad-based background in a number of different job functions may give you an advantage in the organizational climb as compared with someone whose background is solely in the development area.

### Outlook

There have been a number of articles about "the end of programmers" and how 4GLs, prototyping utilities, code generators and form managers, and other tools would mean that end users would be the sole developers and maintainers of information systems. Don't believe it. Although there are far more resources available to end users than in the past, the very nature of complicated information environments such as transaction processing systems requires, at least for the fore-seeable future, a great deal of developer work to start with user-gener-ated screen prototypes and basic code and develop those resources into a real-life information system.

There may, however, be a day, probably many years away, when this vision of end-user generation will become a reality. That is one primary reason why a well-rounded career path, particularly one which gets you close to system users and exposes you to many aspects of the computer field, is important to protect your career options.

### Tip

Standards are becoming a very important part of software develop-ment. The American National Standards Institute (ANSI) and the International Standards Organization (ISO) have a number of stan-dards efforts in such areas as SQL and relational database, dictionar-ies and repositories, and programming languages. Knowledge of and involvement with standards efforts can be an important career booster. Many large user organizations, as well as vendors, have representa-tives to the various standards committees. A good way to become in-volved is to be an internal reviewer at your firm of documents, change proposals, and the other volumes of literature that are generated by the committees and feed input back to your committee representative. After some time, you might be the candidate for membership on new standards committees or take the place of someone on an existing com-mittee.

You can build a large "networking" base of contacts at different com-panies, which can help you both in terms of eventual changes in em-ployment as well as generate business relationships that benefit your current organization. Professional reputation is often greatly enhanced by membership on standards committees, and if you like to travel, you can spend a great deal of your time at committee meetings around the world.

### Systems Analysts

Yes, there are still "plain old systems analysts" in the computer field. As with the traditional programmer, most organizations have chosen to combine the responsibilities of the various portions of the develop-mental lifecycle into broad-based software developers. However, some large, usually *Fortune* 100 level or governmental organizations still make a distinction between those who determine the characteristics of information systems and users' needs and those who actually imple-ment the systems. The former positions are those of the systems analysts, and the latter encompass the developers. Systems analysts can be known by many other job titles: requirements analysts, business analysts, or simply analysts, to name a few. For simplicity, we'll use the term "analyst" for the rest of this section.

Analysts are the primary interface between the current and eventual users of a system and the development staff. Their primary responsibility is to determine, in as detailed a manner as possible, the true needs of the users as well as a prioritized list of nonessential but nice-to-have features and components. Analysts do involve themselves in user interfaces (UIs), including ergonomics of screen design and other UI factors, but either usually do not get involved in or get involved only peripherally in the actual software development. When rapid prototyping tools are available, the analysts may develop UI-based prototypes to facilitate user feedback before costly full-scale implementation, but they likely will not write fully functional computer code, leaving that task to the developers.

Analysts typically produce a set of requirements and specifications, as well as cost-benefit analyses and other documents applicable to the early stages of the development lifecycle. These are verified and validated by the users and others and then turned over to the development staff to design and implement the hardware and software systems.

### Skills for success

A good analyst must be able to distinguish between true user needs and features that would be nice to have but aren't essential to accomplish their missions. In an environment with unlimited development staff resources and unlimited time to implement a system, a comprehensive, endless list of "requirements," all of equal importance, would be a measure of an analyst's worth to an organization. In the real world, especially in recent years with tightly constrained resources, it is the analyst's primary responsibility to *analyze* how users do their jobs and how that can be improved by new or refined computer and communications efforts. As mentioned earlier, a great amount of attention should be given to user interface input and output considerations. A similar degree of detail should be given to determining the required content behind those interfaces and the relative priorities of that content.

A background in *enterprise modeling*—developing data and process models of an organization's current and proposed information and data components—is important to being able to grasp the very complex details of large-scale requirements collection. By using modeling techniques and associated automated tools, an analyst can get a handle on what would otherwise be an overwhelming level of detail.

### Educational background

Successful analysts often have a business-oriented computer background, given the problem of matching user requirements with system characteristics. Most information systems degree programs contain courses in structured analysis and design and similar requirements-oriented subjects. That does not, of course, prevent someone with a computer science or other background from being a successful analyst; rather, such a person is likely to be successful at a "complete" software development position that includes aspects of analysis and development.

### Career progression

Analysts have much the same career paths as software developers: progression into supervisory and management roles. It should be mentioned, however, that an analyst without much practical software development experience may have some difficulty functioning as a software development supervisor or manager. Given that many analysts came to their positions from coding and direct development positions, that critical understanding of the aspects of development is likely to be part of their backgrounds.

### Outlook

Even though, as stated in this section, many organizations still utilize analysts who are divorced from the actual software development, the professionals who combine the skills of requirements analysis and specification, software development, and system testing have a greater chance for career success. Just as software developers should be more than backroom coders, so analysts should try not to operate without software development experience. Hiring organizations look for professionals who can participate in the entire development lifecycle from determining user interfaces and requirements to maintaining and modifying code that is developed as a result from those earlier steps. The broader the background, the greater the chance for career progression.

### Tip

A successful analyst often provides user departments with one of their few links to the computer and communications worlds. Believe it or not, there are still many potential computer users who are terrified of any aspects of automation. There are still, to this day, many cases of systems implementations that have been sabotaged (for lack of a better word) by those who feared that "the computer is here to take our jobs."

Analysts should, when the potential for that type of situation becomes apparent, stress the benefits to users in terms of potential for promotion, career broadening, and other *personal* benefits, rather than "this system will make you twice as productive" or other organizational benefits that mean little to someone afraid of losing his or her job. "Twice as productive" is usually interpreted as "We only need half of you."

## Hardware Engineering and Development

The bulk of this chapter discusses software- and system-oriented positions. The reason is that a majority of the positions in the career field deal with software development, implementing complete systems, and similar areas of responsibility. It is important to remember, however, that without the people who design and develop processors, memory, disks and storage media, network devices, boards, and the other types of computer hardware, there would be nothing for which to write software nor any systems to install and implement.

Unlike software developers, analysts, and consultants, computer hardware professionals are nearly always found at vendors. There are some hardware-oriented opportunities at, for example, aerospace companies that develop satellites with embedded systems, but the vast majority of hardware development is accomplished at computer vendors from IBM to Digital Equipment to Intel to thousands of other companies.

Hardware professionals are also usually true engineers as opposed to my hated "software engineers." By that I mean the people who design and develop hardware are electrical, mechanical, and computer engineers with formal engineering school training as opposed to software developers with business backgrounds who find themselves in positions with the job title of software engineer but who have no engineering background whatsoever. Before anyone takes this personally, I have held several positions over the years with the title of "software engineer," and I no more consider myself a professional engineer than I would think of myself as an astronaut or a surgeon. It takes more than a job title to become a member of a profession.

Anyway, back to the subject at hand. Conventional wisdom holds that there are fewer opportunities for hardware professionals than in the past because of the increasing use of standardized processors, memories, and other components. In reality, the opportunities have just become more distributed than in the past. No longer are most of the hardware positions concentrated at mainframe manufacturers; instead, they are divided among companies that manufacture disks, memory, and other plug-compatible components.

## Skills for success and educational background

Hardware professionals must have a great deal of technical prowess. In my opinion, a majority of people, even noncomputer professionals, can be trained to write software, particularly with the 4GLs, forms managers, and other advanced interfaces available today. However, it takes a great deal of educational background and basic technical aptitude to design a central processing unit or a disk controller.

As mentioned in the preceding portion, hardware professionals are usually engineers by training, with educational backgrounds in electrical, mechanical, or other engineering disciplines. Many have graduate degrees in complementary engineering subjects (e.g., undergraduate degree in electrical engineering or a graduate degree in mechanical engineering). Still others combine engineering and computer science backgrounds. Those who aspire to supervisory and management positions in the hardware area often have some graduate business school training as well.

## Career progression

There are a variety of paths for a hardware professional to follow. As with software developers, some choose to remain hands-on engineers and others aspire to management positions. In the employ of a computer vendor, a hardware professional with a good software background can position himself or herself for a major new development project such as a new hardware technology with a new operating system. Again, most career-advancing opportunities for hardware professionals tend to be at computer vendors, rather than in user organizations, but that doesn't mean that crossover careers don't occur.

## Outlook

The conventional wisdom in the 1980s was that hardware technology was improving in areas of performance, price, and features much more rapidly than software technology. While software productivity struggles to catch up through better CASE tools than in the past, hardware technology continues to march along. That means opportunities in chip design and other hardware-oriented positions are still present.

One thing that has changed from the past decade is the potential for an engineer with an idea to obtain millions of dollars in venture capital to start his or her own firm. The early part of the 1980s was booming with firms making processors, floppy disks, network cards, and hundreds of other types of computer hardware, each struggling to become the de facto standard in an area of technology. Nearly anyone with an idea could get financing and start his or her own company, often in northern California or New England. Given the failures and consolidations among those startups as the decade progressed, financiers are far more cautious now that the winning technologies have been determined. That doesn't mean there no longer are such opportunities nor will there be any in the future; it means instead that the various technologies have matured. As new technologies, possibly biochips and other areas of current research, become commercially feasible, there may be new bursts of venture-driven activity.

**Tip**

As with software development, consulting, and other professions discussed in this chapter, hardware engineers should be aware of the marriage of computer and communications technologies and adapt their careers accordingly. A hardware engineer at a mainframe computer vendor, for example, might be able to survive a corporate shift toward developing distributed smaller systems if he or she has some background in the various communications hardware technologies and how they might be applied to the new corporate direction. Just as real-life software systems don't exist in a vacuum, neither do the hardware systems of the future. Even formerly stand-alone mainframe systems need easy interfaces via channel attachments and other mechanisms to talk with networks of personal computers and workstations.

## Software or Hardware Development Supervisors and Managers

Let me begin this section by stating a fact of which most people in the computer profession are aware: Success as a software developer or hardware engineer has little or no correlation with the ability to be a supervisor or manager of others in those roles. The prototypical career path has always been viewed as progression from developer to senior developer to supervisor to manager to senior manager, or some variation thereof. Career paths are discussed in greater detail in Chap. 5, but it is worth mentioning here that not every hands-on developer, no matter how talented, will succeed in a supervisory or managerial role, nor do some of the whiz kid types who are happiest working with computer code or chips wish to try. As we will see in Chap. 5, many large organizations have realized that over the years and have created dual paths—technical and managerial—to allow people to receive promotions and additional responsibilities without dragging them, kicking and screaming, into positions that require oversight of others.

For those who do aspire to supervisory and managerial positions—which is probably a majority of the readers—we will discuss the types of midlevel management positions. Different organizations have various types of supervisory hierarchies, but the typical development organizational structure looks like that shown in Fig. 3.3. Keep in mind that organizations have different numbers of management layers, but traditionally there is a group development manager who is responsible for all software development within some organizational boundary; it might be by product type at a vendor or by geographic site in a user organization. Underneath that group manager there are a number of development managers, each responsible for a single product or system. Each of the managers usually has one or more supervisors, depending on the size of his or her project, and each supervisor oversees a team of developers that usually ranges in size from two to fifteen. Finally, each team may have a team leader who doesn't have any supervisory responsibilities but instead functions as the chief technical spokesperson for his or her team and works closely with the other team leaders.

Supervisors have the responsibility to establish and manage development schedules for their teams and ensure that potential problems are noted as quickly as possible to facilitate resolution. Some supervisors have technical roles, thereby assuming the responsibilities of team leaders as well as their supervisory tasks; others are strictly involved with development schedules, budgeting, and personnel matters such as staffing and interviewing, performance reviews and appraisals, and vacation scheduling.

The system development managers, who are responsible for entire projects or products, coordinate the management functions of their supervisors and oversee the scheduling, budgeting, and personnel tasks. They also assume political roles more than the supervisors do; they often negotiate with other development managers regarding the inevitable trade-offs that arise in any development effort, particularly when the systems have interfaces with one another. A good system development manager in a vendor organization will also work closely with product managers, marketing and sales managers, training managers, and the other functional managers. Those in user environments will work with user groups, steering committees, and corporate management.

Finally, a group development manager, who is responsible for the success of a number of development efforts, typically is responsible for setting organizational visions and general policies, which are then implemented by his or her staff managers. Examples of these visions and policies would be that all software development must be done in C or Ada, all software must run on both UNIX and OS/2, and that any completed system must have a graphical, window-based user interface.

The group development manager typically works with his or her peers such as the organizational finance director to ensure that all long-range plans developed by the software development organization can be supported through adequate staffing and capital equipment acquisition.

## Skills for success

A successful midlevel manager (we will use this term to indicate anyone from a first-line supervisor up to a group development manager) must, above all, be skilled in managing people. Many talented hardware engineers and software developers tend to be unique in their career aspirations, both short- and long-term, and it is up to the manager to see that their charges' talents are utilized in the way that is best for the organization. Most successful managers practice some form of situational, goals-oriented management, whereby they function in a very task-oriented manner; as long as milestones are met, they don't care if their subordinates work 20 hours straight and then take a day off. Managers who tend to be too rigid in these types of creative environments often find revolts on their hands as their most talented yet temperamental workers choose to work elsewhere.

That doesn't mean that every midlevel manager should take a totally hands-off approach. Situational management means that, in some circumstances, close direction is required. Midlevel managers should be exactly what is implied in the term "managers" as well as leaders. It is important for these managers to have the respect of their workers. Although the further away managers get from the actual design and development work the less technically competent they have to be, developers tend to respect the managers who set reasonable schedules and can make intelligent, sound decisions much more than they do those who operate in a nontechnical vacuum. A manager might not be versed in, for example, the exact nature of parameter passing when developing a mixed 4GL and C application, but he or she should be able to intelligently help decide what languages, databases, development platforms, and other tools are best for his or her projects.

## Educational background

Midlevel managers should have a combination technical and managerial educational background. Note that, in this case, "managerial" is not necessarily the same as "business." The further one wants to progress in software development management the more he or she should have a business background in finance, marketing, and other subjects. At a minimum, good supervisory and management abilities

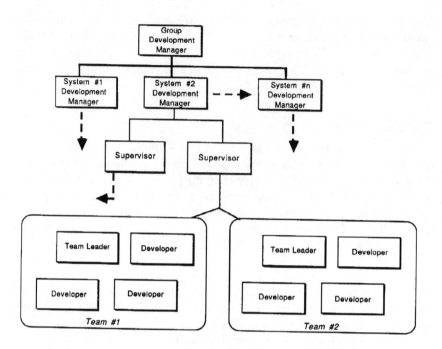

**Figure 3.3** Software development management hierarchy.

are often predicated upon an understanding of basic management techniques, organizational behavior, and similar knowledge.

### Career progression

As illustrated in Fig. 3.3, there is a fairly standard career path from
software or hardware developer to team leader to first-line supervisor
and on up to the various levels of management available within an organization. It should be noted, however, that a rise to top computer
management might be enhanced by moving back and forth among the
various development management levels and positions of equivalent
responsibility in product management or sales (if at a vendor) or in a
noncomputer area such as manufacturing or finance if at a user organization. This concept is discussed further in Chap. 5.

### Outlook

When I was researching for this book in early 1991, a Denver recruiting manager told me that the outlook for first-line supervisors and
managers was somewhat bleak within his client company base. The
reason was that, as organizations struggle to streamline their staffs

and downsize their operations, entire levels of management were being cut. The supervisors and managers who were not only retaining their positions but finding new ones were those who were as technically astute as possible. In times such as these, organizations can no longer afford midlevel managers who simply write performance reviews and coordinate schedules provided by their team leaders. Even though it has always been considered a step backward to move from a business-oriented or management position into a hands-on development position (though I once did that with no regrets), some midlevel managers are being asked to make that transition, and those who have retained their technical skills are the survivors in position-cutting times.

As economies improve and organizations take on new development projects, there will likely be an increasing need for supervisors and managers. The lessons of the late 1980s and early 1990s should not be forgotten, however, and these midlevel managers should try to retain and increase as much technical knowledge as possible.

### Tip

When those under you are involved in disputes of any type, whether technical disagreements with other groups or personnel-based ones such as the amount of an annual raise or a promotion, *always* back them up if you believe they are right. The only type of manager who is more disliked by subordinates than an incompetent one is one who will not stand behind them when they are right. You may not always win on their behalf, but at least you will gain the respect, and likely increased productivity, of your charges, and everyone is likely to benefit in the long run.

### Database Administrators

There are several different computer career positions that specialize in databases and database management systems (DBMS). We've already looked at software development jobs that emphasize development of database applications and environments. For those who enjoy working with databases, a natural career progression would be to specialize in database administration.

A database administrator (DBA) has varying roles, depending on the organization in which he or she works. You likely will be responsible for collecting database requirements as opposed to applications requirements. Database requirements include the number of transactions per second (TPS) that the organization's database must support, as well as backup and recovery requirements, necessary security procedures, and distribution of the data. You would then match these with commercial

DBMS products and work with the organization's information systems management to select one or more database systems.

You are also often responsible for coordiaating and managing data definitions provided by the various applications developers and maintaining close control over records, tables and columns, objects, and the other characteristics of the databases. You will control the utilization of test and production databases and ensure that data integrity is maintained during new releases of both the applications software and the underlying DBMS. There is also involvement with data dictionaries, design tools, and many other areas that deal with your organization's databases.

## Skills for success

It is only natural that a DBA should have a very extensive background in database management systems. Knowledge of the various database models (hierarchical, network, relational, and object-oriented) is very important, especially if you become involved in projects that migrate such as applications that utilize IBM's hierarchical IMS system to those that utilize DB2, Oracle, or another relational product. Experience with the various tools and utilities available—graphical database design tools, performance monitors and tuners, and backup utilities, among others—is also essential to ensure that the database performance is satisfactory and data integrity is maintained.

Knowledge of distributed database technology is important for DBAs as distributed database products become more commercially available than in the past. Even though most DBAs don't develop applications themselves, they often assist the applications programmers with the database programming portions of their codes, including embedded and module SQL, view definitions, transaction design, and other database-oriented components.

## Educational background

A successful DBA might have undergraduate and graduate degrees in either computer science or computer information systems with a curriculum emphasis on databases. Many universities offer a number of different courses in database-related topics. The University of Florida even has a database "subdepartment" within its information sciences program that is staffed by a number of well-published, highly notable professors. When I worked in Digital Equipment's database tools group several years ago, we sponsored some research products at the University of Florida and consulted with one of their highly qualified professors. Anyone with an educational background from their database research group would be well qualified for a position as a database administrator.

### Career progression

Some large organizations have organizational layers of database administrators to manage very large numbers of databases. Large *Fortune* 500 organizations sometimes have hundreds of applications with thousands of tables and hundreds of thousands of columns, which is well beyond the scope of any single individual to manage. A DBA in such an environment can often find a career path within the database organization and eventually move up to supervise or manage other DBAs. Alternatively, some DBAs may move into managing applications development or systems programming staffs, particularly for database-intensive systems.

### Outlook

In the old days (pre-1980), nearly all databases were of the hierarchical or network type or were based on a home-grown linked list and tree structure. All such models required vast support from one or more DBAs, since managing data definitions and other administrative functions was extremely complex and time-consuming. With the advent of relational databases, the role of DBAs, especially in smaller organizations, has somewhat diminished. Relational databases, especially when coupled with dictionaries and repositories that provide data definition support, require less direct DBA management than the older models. There is still a strong role for DBAs, especially in large organizations, because DBMS environments often turn into a case of "a little knowledge is a dangerous thing." Without proper training, many applications developers tend to design and implement databases in the most inefficient way possible; meanwhile, they violate all rules of data normalization and create the database equivalent of spaghetti code. A good DBA can keep problems of that nature from growing into major disasters.

### Tip

A highly qualified DBA should be very aware of such related aspects of information management as dictionaries and repositories, 4GLs that are coupled with underlying databases, and design tools. All these technologies are closely related to the database area, and experience with and knowledge about them can greatly increase a DBA's career options.

## Software Architects

A software architect can be viewed as an organization's focal point for standards. Vendors have software architects to specify callable interfaces, parameters, and other facilities to make their various software products able to work with one another. The advent of such enterprise architectures as IBM's SAA, Hewlett-Packard's New Wave, Computer Associates' CA90, and a host of others has brought about a boom in the vendor-based software architecture business. As vendors struggle to incorporate previously incompatible software products and environments with one another, architects help define the required interfaces between the existing products and the new platforms.

Software architects may also have roles in user organizations, particularly in large corporations. Since user organizations wish to share as much data and information between different departments as possible, software architects can define and support standard interfaces for development environments and platforms across the organization. In that way, individual organizations can use whatever tools and platforms are best suited for their environments as long as they conform to the overall organization's guidelines.

### Skills for success

Software architects can be viewed as "super systems development professionals." Even though they usually don't have direct development responsibilities, they should have strong backgrounds in software technology. Many of the skills that systems analysts should possess, such as interviewing techniques and good written communications, are applicable to software architects also, since software architects function as the systems analysts of the systems programming world by providing requirements and specifications to systems software developers.

### Career progression

Software architecture is a somewhat specialized area, and it tends to be concentrated in large vendor and user organizations. A typical career progression for a software architect might be to a software development supervisor or manager position.

### Outlook

As was mentioned before, the explosion of standards and enterprise architectures has created a great need for software architects at vendor organizations. It is anticipated that opportunities for software architects will continue to grow as the enterprise architectures become reality over the next few years and newer iterations bring additional operating systems, networks, and environments into those architectures.

## Tip

A successful software architect must be astute in organizational politics. Specifying interfaces that affect many different software products is a tricky proposition, and a great deal of care is required to avoid becoming entrenched in interorganizational battles.

## Senior Information Systems Managers

Most computer professionals share the eventual career objective of reaching the ranks of senior information systems management. Such positions include chief information officer (CIO), vice-president of information systems, president or executive vice-president at a computer hardware, software, or services company, or other roles with similar levels of responsibility.

Senior IS managers are usually responsible for organizations ranging from several hundred to thousands of people, research and development budgets sometimes reaching into the billions of dollars, and other lofty corporate assets. It is no wonder, then, that corporate boards of directors and other hiring authorities are very particular in the characteristics and backgrounds of those to whom they entrust such responsibility.

It should be immediately pointed out that at the level of organizational management we are discussing, such items as educational background are somewhat inapplicable. Most business schools would have you believe that an MBA is essential for the rise to the corporate boardroom, but the plain truth is that although a business education background doesn't hurt, it isn't essential to achieve the ultimate corporate success. Many of the senior executives in the information systems professionals are entrepreneurs with a much stronger technical than business background, and they know the secrets of delegating the business authority to other senior executives while they set the technical directions of their firms.

It might also be surprising that a strong, in-depth technical background is not necessarily essential either. You will find chief financial officers, executive vice presidents, chief operating officers, and others throughout senior information systems management who started their careers in areas other than computers or communications and made the successful switch into the computer field at some point.

How do you reach the senior ranks of information systems management, given that the role models have such diverse backgrounds? There are a number of factors, including:

1. *Hard work and self-sacrifice.* As in any industry, most senior executives have held series of positions of increasing levels of responsibility and authority. Most of those positions required long hours, extensive travel, separations from families, and other aspects of conflict between business and personal lives. Not every computer professional is suited to the responsibilities of a senior management position, *nor does every highly qualified person aspire to the road to that level.* An important part of the insight aspect discussed in the first chapter deals with more than just knowing which areas of the computer field you might be best at; it is also important to know exactly what your career aspirations are with respect to the organization levels to which you aspire. Many professionals in all types of career fields are taking a long look inside themselves after the go-go, career-oriented years of the 1980s and making the determination that they want to spend more time with their families, hobbies, and other noncareer aspects of their lives than the climb to corporate management would permit. There is nothing wrong with either possibility, but it should be recognized that the road to the upper executive levels may not be for everyone, including some professionals who would make excellent senior managers.

2. *Understanding the aspects of organizational politics.* Organizational politics exists at every level within every corporation, not-for-profit group, and governmental organization. Any executive who desires to climb the organizational ladder must be aware of his or her organizational political climate, such as understanding who holds the reigns of power and what the acceptable and unacceptable behaviors and norms are in that organization. Many technically oriented computer people would look at the above sentences and think, "That's ridiculous; technical merit and other such factors should be the determinants in who receives promotions and additional responsibility." Without sounding too sarcastic, for anyone of that mindset, that's not how the real world works. A utopian world might have the most technically competent people who are the best managers and motivators rising to the top of organizations, but in real life, there are uncountable cases in which organizational political factors far outweigh the other qualifications or lack thereof of those competing to get ahead. However, it should also be noted that the computer field is full of many very good senior executives as well, so no one should assume that a manager is at his or her level solely because of an ability to leverage political assets. Every manager should be judged on his or her success and results in positions of responsibility.

3. *Career insight.* In addition to the insight, mentioned above, about how high one might wish to try to climb on the organizational ladder, successful senior executives tend to have a great deal of insight with respect to advancing technologies, companies and organizations, the

correct career paths to pursue in their own situations, and the other aspects of computer career success discussed in the first chapter. They do not hesitate to do what is best for their careers, nor do they let mistakes become too entrenched before taking corrective action.

## Product Managers

Nearly all firms that develop and sell hardware and software—that is, vendors—utilize the skills of product managers to coordinate a number of functions of product development and introduction. Product managers typically work closely with a variety of other managers, including those responsible for development, marketing, sales, training, legal protection, and customer support, as well as the company's other products.

Let's look at a hypothetical software firm, DB Corp., that develops and markets computer-aided software engineering (CASE) tools in the database design area, and we'll see what that firm's product managers do in the course of their jobs. Assume that DB Corp. currently has one product on the market, a performance optimizer for IBM's DB2 database management system. DB Corp. decides to develop and market a tool that will allow users to use a workstation and conceptually design databases by electronically drawing and manipulating entity relationship (ER) diagrams. DB Corp. then hires you to be the manager for this new product and gives you a general charter to manage the product introduction function.

First, understand that, in most organizations, the product management function is *not* the same as that of managing the product development. The latter function falls to software or hardware development supervisors and managers, whose positions we looked at earlier. The product manager usually acts as a coordinating manager of the various functions—finance, marketing, sales, and the others mentioned earlier in this section—but doesn't have any line management control over those other managers.

In this particular circumstance, your new assignment as a product manager will require you to collect and coordinate product requirements for the ER design tool from a variety of sources, including competitors' product literature, technical papers and publications, consultants, conferences, and—possibly most important—interviews and meetings with customers and potential users. Together with the product marketing personnel, you will likely meet with current customers of DB Corp. to determine what product features they would like to see in your firm's tool, how they would like to see that tool interface with your existing product, and what characteristics of the product's user interface (types of windows, mouse and keyboard control, sequences of actions, etc.) they would like to see.

Once a set of requirements is developed, you will meet with the software development manager to jointly develop a product specification, which, after coordination with the other DB Corp. functional managers, will be used by the software development manager to create design specifications, staffing plans, and development schedules. Meanwhile, you will work with the marketing manager to develop marketing strategies and product introduction plans, including product positioning, pricing, target market analysis, and other general marketing functions. The marketing managers will then take the general marketing strategy and develop a more comprehensive plan, including trade show participation and other specific functions.

Sales forecasts will be developed along with the sales managers, and they will be used with the pricing information to develop return on investment (ROI) estimates and other financial calculations with the finance specialists.

Meanwhile, you will develop a general intellectual property protection strategy that includes trade secret protection and policies for copyright, patent, and trademark registration. These will then be passed on to DB Corp.'s inside or outside legal organization for action.

You will also need to develop general training plans for customers, customer support specialists, and DB Corp.'s sales staff. The plans will then be coordinated with DB Corp.'s training manager, who will direct his or her staff to develop the specific courses.

As product manager, you will coordinate product testing, customer support, and a number of other functions. Most of the preceding tasks are also a very iterative process requiring constant revision and coordination among DB Corp.'s managers. Integration requirements with DB Corp.'s performance optimizer product must be developed with that product's product manager, who is responsible for ensuring that the requested features are included in a timely manner in the product.

By now, you should be getting the idea that a product manager is the nerve center of product development and introduction efforts in most organizations. Nearly every one of your job functions requires iterative coordination with one or more internal managers, as well as a number of outside customers. Vendors often assign product management teams to major, bet-your-business product efforts, and the teams then divide the aforementioned responsibilities. A product manager is at the very center of product development, and the job can be very interesting and exciting, if tiring.

### Skills for success

A product manager should have as broad a range of skills as possible in technical, business, and interpersonal areas. It is extremely important for a product manager to be as technically astute as possible when meeting with customers and when collecting product requirements. His or her general business skills in marketing, finance, and sales are obviously very important, because the product manager usually develops the first iterations of financial figures, sales and marketing plans, and the legal protection strategy. More than for most computer professionals, a broad-based background and array of technical and business skills is very important for success.

Of course, possession of verbal and written skills, as well as interpersonal negotiating skills, also is very important.

### Educational background

Chapter 6 describes in detail a representative educational background for a software product manager and how it relates to a product manager's career success.

### Career progression

There are a number of career paths a product manager might take. In many large vendor organizations, a move into senior software development management is considered the "smart" career move. In others, logical progression might be toward marketing management. For larger firms, managing other product managers (e.g., a "product management manager") is a straightforward career step.

### Outlook

Although many larger organizations seem to be consolidating product management functions into a lesser number of positions, there is still a strong outlook for product managers in today's and tomorrow's computer job market. New products and versions of existing products are constantly being introduced, and vendors are intensely porting existing products to new (for their applications) operating systems such as OS/2 and UNIX or to platforms such as IBM's Systems Applications Architecture (SAA), all of which often require new product managers for the growing variety of existing products.

Good product managers are difficult to find, given the desirability of a broad-based business and technical background. If, as is emphasized throughout this book, you strive to acquire as broad a background as possible, you might consider spending some time in a product management position.

### Tip

It is very important for a product manager to be able to recognize and work within organizational political climates. Because of the vast degree of interaction, a product manager must be constantly aware of turf wars and personality conflicts and overcome them to the best of his or her ability for the benefit of the organization and its products.

## OIS Specialists and Managers

An OIS specialist or manager crosses several of the job functions visited in this chapter. Often these positions have elements of systems analysis, software development, and networks and communications responsibilities. OIS professionals design and build systems that contain *horizontal* productivity applications—those that cross most user industry boundaries—as opposed to vertical applications, which tend to be industry-specific. Examples of OIS applications include:

Word processing

Spreadsheet

Database, particularly personal computer DBMS products

Graphics

Desktop publishing

Calendar and schedule management

Electronic mail

### Skills for success

A successful OIS specialist should have a strong background in personal computers (since many productivity packages run on PCs), networks, and user interface techniques, as well as have a thorough understanding of office workflows and productivity techniques.

Most OIS components will soon be introducing elements of multimedia computing—voice input and output, image processing, document scanning, and video—in a more widespread manner than today. If you choose to specialize in office information systems, you should have some knowledge of the building blocks used in multimedia applications (see Chap. 8 for more information) and how an organization's productivity can be enhanced through incorporation of those techniques into OIS.

### Educational background

An OIS professional is likely to have either a business-oriented information systems or computer science background.

### Career progression

Alternatives for OIS professionals include working with vendors that produce OIS products or specializing in OIS consulting.

## Outlook

The 1980s began with widespread predictions of office automation and "the paperless organization." Although user organizations of all sizes have extensively utilized personal computers and productivity software, office systems still have a great deal of potential as new workstations, networks, servers, and other technology moves into mainstream office environments. Many organizations are overhauling their first attempts at OIS environments and moving toward a second-generation office environment in an attempt to increase productivity even further than they already have. Therefore, this specialty is one to strongly consider, especially for those attempting to diversify and jump-start their careers.

## Tip

Systems integration skills (see Chap. 8) are very important to OIS environments. Many organizations desire to use a word processing package from vendor A, a calendar system from vendor B, and so on. Experience with integration software and the ability to write "glue routines" is extremely valuable for OIS specialists. Also, many OIS packages allow customization of menus through programming script interfaces, so software development expertise should be another available resource.

## Computer Consultants

To adequately describe the job functions, background, and characteristics of successful computer consultants would take an entire book. In fact, my first book, *How to Be a Successful Computer Consultant,* does exactly that. We will briefly discuss the major components of computer consulting as a career choice in the context of this chapter and this book. In the interest of space conservation, however, we will not get too in-depth in such subjects as how to offer a seminar or the marketing and financial aspects of running your own consulting business, since those topics are discussed in great detail in the aforementioned book.

As layoffs and the other factors we discussed in the last chapter continue, computer consulting is becoming the occupation of choice for more and more computer professionals for two major reasons. First, it is increasingly difficult for many of those who are newly unemployed in the computer career field to find equivalent positions in other organizations because of widespread staff reductions in both vendor and user organizations. Since some companies have chosen to soften their reductions with generous severance packages, many laid-off workers use the financial settlements as seed money to begin consulting practices.

Second, much of the applications development backlog and other computer-related work in the newly streamlined organizations is still there, is critical to the success and growth of the company, *and can't possibly be handled solely by the remaining in-house staff.* It is true that some projects—new or modified applications and some new hardware procurements—are being canceled or delayed by some user organizations, but for the most part computing requirements remain, and user management often chooses to utilize outside resources.

Computer consultants perform a wide variety of functions ranging from contract-based software development for a given application to plotting an information systems course for a *Fortune* 500 corporation's next 5 years. Almost any of the job functions explored in this chapter can provide the basis around which a consulting practice could be built. For example, if you have a strong track record in computer hardware and software sales, you may consider starting a consulting firm that specializes in training, evaluating, and improving the results of vendors' sales staffs.

Some computer professionals have an interest in consulting and the characteristics of the profession—a wide range of clients, frequently changing assignments, and the ability to stay abreast of new technology—but don't wish to start and run their own businesses. In those cases, aligning with existing consulting firms, on either a full-time employment or subcontract basis, is a way to be involved in the consulting area without the overhead of running a business operation. Opportunities exist in the Big 6 (formerly the Big 8) accounting firms, all of which have management and information systems consulting operations, as well as a wide number of regional and national consulting organizations that specialize exclusively in computer consulting.

### Skills for success

It takes more than hanging a shingle that says "The Consultant Is In" to be successful as a computer consultant. Prospective clients look for more than just technical expertise in consultants they hire, since they are potentially committing large sums of money in exchange for critical services. Clients usually look for:[2]

1. *Someone who understands the general principles of a client's business.* In order to propose a solution to a business's problems or opportunity, you need to understand the intricacies of a client's business. That is not to say that prior to your first meeting with your prospective client you must know his or her business intimately, because many businesses conduct their operations in a nonstandard manner or consider certain information more important than similar

businesses do. You should, however, know what a "standard" company in that industry does and be able to discuss business operations intelligently.

2. *Someone who speaks the language of the business.* Your clients are likely to question your capabilities if you require a translation of every industry-specific acronym or term used.

3. *Someone who knows when to use technical computer jargon (and when not to).* Discussions vary widely when you are talking with end users or with another information systems professional. If you are designing a small UNIX-based local area network for a real estate office, your discussions should center around the real estate system's functionality and how it will solve business problems. However, if you are consulting with a computer center manager about which flavor of UNIX on which he or she should standardize the center's new workstations, discussions of kernels, shells, and graphical interfaces are applicable and necessary.

4. *Someone who proposes sensible, cost-effective solutions.* Not every client needs state-of-the-art processors, software, and other technology. Your solutions should be cost-effective, yet still allow for future growth without having to start each iteration over from the beginning.

5. *Someone who appears to be a business person.* This doesn't mean that every meeting should be conducted in a custom-tailored suit. You should dress according to the dress code of your respective clients because they will feel more comfortable talking to someone who is similarly attired. As with any other computer position that deals with clients and other businesses, remember that you are representing your business or organization and to be as professional as possible.

Other characteristics of successful computer consultants include:[3]

1. *Objectivity.* As a consultant, you might often find yourself in the middle of power struggles and other organizational political battles. You should try, as hard as possible, to stay out of these struggles and be as objective as possible in all recommendations.

2. *Creativity.* Clients often look to consultants for solutions to tough problems or to provide new and inventive means with which to take advantage of an opportunity. Consultants shouldn't propose and implement the same solutions over and over, since technology and the business climate change so rapidly.

3. *Integrity.* Since most consultants, with the exception of internal consultants, are outsiders to their clients' organizations, confidentiality in business matters and other inside information is crucial to professional reputations.

### Educational background

Anyone wishing to build his or her own consulting practice should have a sound background in two important business areas. First, marketing is crucial to identifying target markets, determining pricing strategies, and promoting your business. Second, financial skills are critical, since so much of building and running a business revolves around income statements, balance sheets, and—perhaps most important for internal business operations—analyzing cash flow.

A consultant who chooses to emphasize a particular applications area *might* have formal education, possibly a graduate or undergraduate degree, in that area. For example, if you choose to build your practice around accounting information systems or computer auditing, you might be a certified public accountant (CPA) and have a degree in accounting to accompany a management information systems degree. It is less important, however, to have a particular educational background than to have a demonstrated track record of success in that area, a premise that is also true of every other job explored in this chapter as well.

Finally, a computer science or business-oriented information systems degree (see Chap. 6) is almost a 100 percent prerequisite (though, of course, there are exceptions) for applications-oriented or systems-oriented consulting work such as helping to streamline database operations or develop contract software.

### Career progression

Perhaps more than the other positions discussed in this chapter, computer consulting doesn't have one set career path (a subject explored more in the next chapter). A consultant working in a Big 6 accounting firm or other large organization might have a somewhat defined path into consulting management, but those working for themselves—including me—often jump back and forth between working in another organization and solo work. In addition, consultants often revise their technical specialties and services as market conditions evolve.

Consultants are often more able to switch among, and even overlap, a variety of activities and specialties such as seminars, software development, and writing than someone in a fairly rigid career path. Particularly in climates such as those discussed in Chap. 2, consulting and other outside contract work provides a hedge against sudden loss of income that is due to layoffs or other downsizing measures. The career path of Donald Jacobs—the Career Success Profile in Chap. 5—is a perfect example of how to tailor career moves toward industry and technology trends as well as personal objectives.

## Outlook

It might be a bit of an oversimplification, but consultants can succeed in both prosperous times and in less-than-lucrative environments through the factors briefly touched upon here: being recognized as an expert, having a demonstrated record of accomplishment, and providing situational outside resources to a variety of organizations. Most projections for the computer consulting market for the next 5 to 10 years indicate strong growth potential for those in the field. It is best to keep in mind, however, that success is more than just calling yourself a consultant; instead, it requires a wide variety of skills and more than a little perseverance.

## Tip

Always have a backup set of services, applications specialties, and other offerings to anticipate market changes. When I began consulting part-time in 1982 while still a U.S. Air Force officer, my intentions were to concentrate on personal computer software training. As that market became quickly saturated, I rapidly switched to an emphasis on microcomputer database applications development. You should continually review, and if necessary, revise your business plans.

## Computer Operations Managers

Many of you familiar primarily with personal computers and workstations are often surprised to learn that the computer operations function is still a very important part of most large organizations with mainframe-based data processing environments. Although most newer mainframes require less operator support than older systems, there is still a need for staff support for functions such as tape mounting and dismounting, device control, system reconfiguration, network management, and similar tasks. For purposes of this book, however, we won't discuss the actual job of computer operator. Instead, we will briefly discuss the position of computer operations manager.

It should be noted that as smaller, decentralized computers with powerful systems and performance management utilities become the norm, the need for computer operations managers is likely to decrease. Therefore, you should consider very carefully whether operations is an option around which to build your own career path. Nevertheless, since most large organizations still have IBM, UNISYS, Honeywell, Digital, and other mainframes in place, hands-on operations will still be important in the near future.

Operations managers are also the focal points of disaster preparedness and recovery planning and execution. The more critical a computing environment is to the functioning of an organization, the more cru-cial those functions are. Many banking, defense, utility, and other en-vironments in which downtime is disastrous—and sometimes life-threatening—have large operations staffs that heavily emphasize failover management and other recovery techniques. Successful opera-tions managers must be aware of and involved with these activities.

### Skills for success

Operations managers must have strong personnel management skills, since they often supervise staffs of varying sizes. Some senior opera-tions managers oversee groups at multiple locations, which are some-times distributed internationally. Since operator errors can often bring the most sophisticated information processing and telecommunications environments to screeching halts, operations managers must ensure that their charges are thoroughly trained and continue to be proficient in all necessary skills.

### Educational background

Typically, operations managers have backgrounds in computer science or general computer technology, sometimes from a community college or trade school. Knowledge of hardware and software from an opera-tional sense is important, and their educational backgrounds should provide a basis for that knowledge.

### Outlook

As was mentioned previously, the trend towards decentralized, "self-managed" environments is likely to cap the growth in the operations area. A recommendation would be for operations managers to ensure that they have career contingency plans in the event that their organi-zations choose to evolve away from a computer center environment toward easy-care departmental midrange and personal computer envi-ronments.

### Tip

Have a good rapport with the software development staff and other in-formation systems professionals in your organization. Then events such as unexpected downtime and unavailability of resources won't de-generate into antagonistic situations in which the software staff blames operations for missed deadlines, operations blames the pro-grammers for repeatedly crashing the production systems, and so on. Such situations can then be handled in a professional manner with the common goal of supporting the computing mission of the organization as the focal point of problem resolution.

## Sales Professionals

In many vendor organizations, sales professionals are among the most highly compensated staff members. In good years, hardware and software sales staff members with lucrative accounts can earn as much or more than the firm's senior executives. In other organizations, however, the sales staff may be paid on only a salary basis or have a ceiling on the variable portion (i.e., commission) portion of their compensation.

Selling computer hardware, software, and services is in many ways similar to other types of industrial sales from electronic components to financial products and services. The salesperson must meet or exceed quotas established by his or her firm, develop and qualify new business prospects, and service an established customer base. A sales professional may be assigned to a particular customer as an account manager or to a particular industry such as banking with the primary mission of building and fortifying his or her products' entrenchments in the customer base. Others may concentrate more on building new clients in a wide variety of industries, subsequently turning over the newly established accounts to other members of the sales team while he or she moves on to new challenges. The latter falls more in the realm of *business development,* and can also be very rewarding, both in terms of compensation and in career progression.

Sales professionals often do more than just contact prospective or existing customers about new hardware, software, or service products. They are often attached to *bid and proposal* efforts for government and large industrial procurements, matching their firms' offerings with specialized technology requests. Assume that the U.S. Navy has published a request for proposals (RFP) for an office information system (OIS) for a certain naval hospital. Defense contractors that specialize in OISs will compete for this particular procurement, and they will often build proposed systems that include hardware and software from many different vendors. It would be your responsibility as a sales professional to develop business agreements with a selected bidder (or, in many cases, more than one bidder), choose the appropriate hardware, software, and services to be included in the proposal system, and establish the pricing based on profit requirements, strategic objectives (such as account penetration), competitive factors, and other considerations.

You will also request and manage support staff members and company resources for test system demonstrations. That usually includes requisitioning demonstration hardware, coordinating any prototype software development, and managing your firm's participation in the testing competition, as well as the rest of the proposal effort. Following successful efforts, you will then function as the order taker and front-line interface for installation and verification of your firm's products as well as negotiate any contract modifications such as substituting newer products than those specified by the contract.

### Skills for success

Any sales professional, whether in the computer field or in any other industry, should be viewed by customers as a charismatic, knowledgeable, and, above all, trustworthy person. Some people seem to have a natural ability for the sales profession and could successfully build a career selling anything from vacuum cleaners or hot tubs to real estate or computer software. Nearly everyone, however, has encountered a sales person at one time in some setting who appears very uncomfortable with his or her role and seems to be following a mental sales script or flowchart. Anyone who wishes to be successful in sales should be perceived as *truly believing* in his or her products.

In the computer sales field, technical knowledge is very important. I've known some sales professionals who had spent time in a technical role and had in-depth knowledge—which was conveyed to the customer—of hardware and software, both their own and their competitors products. Others have had to rely solely on sales support staff, product managers, and others for anything more technical than a product name and price. As with product managers and other positions discussed in this chapter, a salesperson who can combine technical and business knowledge with the particular skills required for his or her job can be light-years ahead of others in terms of success both in his or her own career and for his or her company's products and services.

International sales can be an interesting variation for sales staff members as trade barriers between nations continue to be reduced. For sales professionals involved in direct sales or sales management in an international environment, additional skills such as foreign language fluency, understanding export and import requirements and restrictions, a general international business background, and cultural training are valuable skills to possess.

### Educational background

A background that includes computer training—either computer science or a business-oriented program—and with a formal business education with a strong emphasis on sales and marketing is a good one for a computer sales professional. It is not a firm prerequisite, however, because one's skills and performance in the sales arena count more than knowledge per se. However, when selling database software, for example, it helps to be able to talk knowledgeably to technically oriented customers about transactions per second rates, null field handling, index structures, and conceptual data modeling rather than just run through a list of product features. Since a sales professional is often the front-line support person for customer relations, it usually gives the customer confidence to know that his or her sales person can provide some direct answers rather than have to go to support personnel for responses to every inquiry.

An understanding of human psychology and organizational behavior also is useful, since prospective customers (as well as nearly everyone else) often make decisions for many reasons other than purely technical or financial. Insight into peoples' decision-making processes can be invaluable in knowing which "buttons to push" to pursue or close a sale.

### Career progression

Just as many engineers and software developers choose to remain in technical areas rather than progress into management, many sales professionals love the process of finding, prospecting, and closing business sales and have no desire to move into sales management positions. Given the high commission-enhanced income that many sales people can receive in prosperous times, they are happy to remain in direct selling roles.

Others who do wish to move to management often find structures that include sales supervisors and regional, district, and national sales managers. Some large vendors have many layers of sales management, which has its positive and negative points; as management levels build in the sales management area, organizations often see diminishing returns that are due to the bureaucracies, turf building, and territorial fighting.

### Outlook

Some organizations have been streamlining their sales staffs in recent years, but most of the reductions have been in layers of sales management or in direct sales staffers who have consistently not met assigned quotas. Opportunities are still readily available for sales professionals with demonstrated track records of consistently exceeding quotas and developing new business for their companies.

### Tip

In addition to knowing your own products thoroughly, you should have an in-depth knowledge of associated products, including those of other companies. If, for example, you sell CASE tools that include SQL code generation among the products' functions, you should be familiar with the DBMS products for which code can be generated, the hardware platforms and operating systems on which those products can run, and third-party data dictionaries and repositories with which the DBMS products and your CASE tools can interoperate. The secret is to convey to your customers that you are providing knowledge about a *total solution,* rather than just point products, that includes offerings from other vendors. Even if your firm doesn't have reselling agreements with other companies, joint bids and programs are often a way to build symbiotic business relations among vendors.

## Customer and Technical Support Specialists

Over the years, I have met some very warped individuals (just joking) who enjoy the ultimate challenge of "busting dumps," analyzing and correcting problems in customers' software, and using line analyzers to figure out why a communications circuit isn't working. These individuals have little or no desire to develop new hardware or software or even to do such "routine maintenance and modification" as adding new features or fixing previously reported problems. Their ultimate challenge is receiving a report of a problem and coming up with an answer to why it occurred and if indeed it is a problem. When I was an Air Force officer, part of my responsibilities for the first three years was a sort of customer support function: responding to emergency problems on one of the warning systems at the North American Air Defense Command (NORAD) in Colorado Springs. Although I personally wouldn't choose again to analyze operator logs, dumps, and input-output recordings while colonels and generals are waiting for an answer, some people in the computer field find that sort of job function to be much more challenging than routine development or the other types of positions described in this chapter.

Many large vendor organizations have a series of customer support centers that perform initial customer support via long-distance through network hookups and the uploading and downloading of necessary information. A customer support specialist in this type of environment is usually assigned one or more software or hardware products for which he or she is the first line of support. Some important customer accounts are assigned their own customer support staff by a vendor. On-site work is often an important part of a support specialist's job, which usually requires frequent travel with little advance notice.

## Skills for success

A support specialist should not only be an expert in the products he or she supports but should also be well versed in symbolic debuggers, communications line analyzers, operating systems utilities, and the other tools of the problem analysis trade. Those who support older systems and don't have and never will have a wide range of tools (as I once did, on a Sperry 1100/42) must be able to read register and memory dumps as well as be able to understand object code listings obtained from compilations.

A checklist orientation mentality might be applied to some support positions, but the ability to be innovative and search out all possible paths in the problem resolution process is critical. Some problems are repeats of previously reported ones, but they tend to be fixed through software patches or similar means and be applied to all users of the hardware or software. The next round of problems will probably be very different and require a different analysis path.

Customer support specialists also work with the developers of the hardware and software when necessary, usually when actual source code must be analyzed to determine problem causes.

## Educational background

A strong computer science background is very important for customer support people. That is not to say that you can't be successful without that type of educational background, since when I supported hardware, networks, and systems software, I had a business information systems background and learned nearly all of what I needed on the job. A good foundation in operating systems architectures, compilers, networks and communications, and other techniques is very helpful, though. Much of the precise technical knowledge required comes from vendor-specific training, but experience in other systems through an educational background can be important to career progression.

## Career progression

Some customer support specialists move into positions that manage a support staff. Others, as with many software developers and hardware engineers, prefer to remain in technical hands-on positions.

## Outlook

Even though the trend over the past decade or so has been toward hardware and software that is easier to analyze, customer support is still a very important part of any vendor's service offerings. Many large user organizations also have their own support staffs who attempt to resolve problems in-house before they work with the vendors. There should be steady growth for the specialists involved in the hands-on support. As with other positions discussed in this chapter, however, the many layers of customer support management are dwindling at many vendors, and growth should be somewhat more restrained in that area.

### Tip

Always try to find the true cause of problems you are investigating. I remember a number of problems I investigated in the past that appeared to have a certain cause which was fixed, only to have those problems occur again. Before you pronounce a problem fixed, make sure that it really is, because your reputation can suffer from too many false cures.

## Data Communications and Telecommunications Specialists

We previously discussed software development professionals who specialize in writing communications device drivers, protocol handlers, and other software that is communication-oriented in nature. A rapidly growing specialty is working in areas that cross the boundaries between the computer and telecommunications industries. In the past, there was a somewhat firm distinction between data processing and teleprocessing. The growth of decentralized, distributed, and mixed data-voice-video systems has blurred the distinctions. Many professionals remain involved solely with computer systems or telecommunications, but more and more positions require an understanding of and expertise in both areas.

A communications specialist might be one who designs wide area networks (WANs) or local area networks (LANs), or one who actually does the network installation, including cabling, connecting computers to the network media, configuring telephone interfaces, and other mixed computer-telecommunication tasks. Because of our well-discussed slowdown in employment, organizations *highly* value someone with skills in as many of these areas as possible.

### Skills for success

A communications specialist must be versed in both hardware and software, particularly that which has to do with the information processing networks. That includes gateways and bridges, protocol drivers, network interface devices, and network-based application and system software. Troubleshooting skills also are valuable, since even the simplest local area networks often require a bit of refinement to operate correctly and efficiently.

### Educational background

There is still something of a lack of practical, hands-on educational programs in communications. Most computer science and information systems programs have courses in data communications, but few have hands-on experience with satellite communications, LANs, and writing a protocol handler. Fortunately, many of the continuing education companies that sponsor seminars feature these types of courses for networks and other communications areas.

### Career progression

Someone with a solid background in both computer and communications technology has a wide range of career options available. New network architectures and products are constantly being introduced and upgraded. The rush toward system integration (see Chap. 8) has provided great opportunities for those who are versed in bridges, routers, gateways, and other connectivity products. Consulting is a popular option, as is senior information systems management.

### Outlook

The systems integration and heterogeneous connectivity trends mentioned in Chap. 2, together with client-server products, distributed databases, and other mixed-technology areas, provides this area with *one of the strongest growth potentials of all the positions discussed in this chapter.* Networks and communications are becoming one of the major distinguishing characteristics between old and new technologies—and those involved with those technologies—in a number of areas.

### Tip

Network and communications technology, features, and prices change much more rapidly than operating systems, compilers, database models, and other computer-specific areas. If you are specializing in this area, staying as technologically current as possible is as crucial as for any other type of position discussed in this chapter. See Chap. 9 for more information on staying on top of technology.

## Technical Writers

One of the long-standing perceptions in the computer industry is that developers and engineers are, for the most part, horrible writers. In reality, there is some truth to that, but it should also be understood that some talented technical people can communicate as well. (And they are the people who usually advance up organizational ladders into upper management.)

Even when a technical staffer can also write, it is rare that the person who writes code or designs a disk drive will write the user and technical support documentation for the products. Most organizations utilize technical writers to perform the documentation function.

A technical writer takes input from the technical staff—internal design documents, outlines of documentation, screen prototypes, and other sources—and develops various types of documentation. Anyone who has purchased a PC software package usually finds a user's guide, a one- or two-volume reference manual, an installation guide, and assorted other documentation. Each of these documentations has a different orientation in terms of its content and how it is organized. Similar documentation is used internally by the trainers and educators, customer support staff, and others. It is the responsibility of the technical writers to ensure that the appropriate form and content are used in all applicable types of documentation.

### Skills for success

The most obvious skill of a successful technical writer is the ability to communicate on paper. Most readers have seen examples of poorly written documentation that is of little or no help to its readers, and sometimes can even be damaging because of incorrect content.

### Educational background

Technical writers don't necessarily have to have degrees in English, literature, or some other writing-intensive curriculum. Some technical writers come from development backgrounds; they have the desire to write something other than computer programs and internal code comments. There is no standard background for a technical writer because demonstrated communications ability carries far more weight in qualifying someone for a job in this area than a particular set of courses taken in college or elsewhere.

### Career progression

Vendors usually have technical writing organizations, and as with customer support, education and training, and other support functions there is some form of management structure. As with these other functions as well, these managements have been somewhat streamlined in recent years.

## Outlook

The model that many vendors are trying to adopt is that of Apple Computer: the less documentation the better. Vendors are trying to get away from the 30-volume reference sets for the operating system, accompanied by a 12-volume set for each product. The more complex the hardware and the more full-featured the software, of course, the richer the documentation set must be, but the trend is to try to avoid repeating the same explanation of, say, a database SELECT command in ten different places. Regardless of the user manual picture, there is still the need for customer support and other internal documents. Therefore, hands-on, skilled technical writers are likely to have tasks to do. Technical writing is also a perfect specialty with which to set up a consulting or contract work business, because many vendors are going outside for documentation work to save on full-time staff resources.

## Tip

Try to know as much as possible about the technology behind the products for which you are doing documentation. When you are writing a relational database reference manual, for example, the document throughput will be greatly increased if you understand the concepts of schemas, normalization, tables and columns, join operations, and other database technical material rather than have to constantly seek technical assistance.

## University and College Professors

The term "professor" in this section refers to any tenure-track or tenured associate professor, assistant professor, or full professor. Tenure is a concept in academia that provides a number of job and academic benefits including a measure of job security, voting rights on college and university matters, and others.

Anyone who has been to college is familiar with the primary tasks of a professor, which are to teach undergraduate and graduate classes and provide student academic counseling. Most people who have obtained a graduate degree are aware of a number of other responsibilities such as supervising graduate students and their research, conducting seminars, and obtaining research grant funding from a wide range of sources.

There are a number of trade-offs to an academic career in the computing field. On the positive side, schedules are fairly flexible with respect to class dates and times, office hours, and other responsibilities, which allows a greater deal of freedom than in many corporate environments. Exposure and reputation can be obtained more readily through publications, presenting research results and conferences and seminars, and other public appearances. Professors usually are involved with state-of-the-art technology through their research, and they have a great deal of freedom as to the areas in which to do their research work. Visiting professorships are readily obtainable, often in foreign countries, without having to forsake current university affiliations.

On the negative side, however, salaries tend to stagnate for all but the superstars once the upper academic levels are reached. That must be taken in context, however, since most published salaries tend to be for *9-month academic years only*. Additional earnings are possible through summer school instruction, research grant funding, writing, and outside consulting. For example, a published salary of $45,000 for an assistant professor might in actuality be doubled, as shown in Table 3.1. In addition, since many professors often write high-priced textbooks that they and their colleagues require their students to have for their courses, total annual income can often stretch well into six figures.

**TABLE 3.1   Composition of Academic Compensation**

| | |
|---|---:|
| Base salary, 9-month academic year | $45,000 |
| Visiting summer school professorship, 2 courses | 6,000 |
| Publication of three articles in trade journals | 4,500 |
| Research funds | 10,000 |
| Seminar fees | 10,000 |
| Consulting fees | 10,000 |
| Total compensation | $85,000 |

### Skills for success

Any college or university professor should strive to be an unequaled expert in whatever areas of computer technology he or she chooses as an emphasis, such as databases, compilers, operating systems, or graphics. In addition, an extremely strong background in as many areas of hardware, software, and communications technology is essential to round out the base knowledge from which instruction is formulated.

### Educational background

Chapter 6 discusses in more detail an optimal educational background for a professor. For career progression, a doctoral degree is a must. Those without doctoral degrees are usually (but not always) relegated to nontenured positions such as "visiting instructor" or adjunct professor. Although such positions are more than suitable for those who are pursuing part-time teaching, those who wish to emphasize their careers in academia should strive to be on a tenure track.

### Career progression

The classic career progression in academia is to begin as an associate or assistant professor and work your way into a full, tenured professorship. Departmental chairman is a career goal of some full professors, whereas others wish to concentrate on their classroom work, research, and outside activities rather than manage an entire department.

Some choose to advance through the university administration ladder and receive appointments as deans of colleges and academic vice presidents of such areas as student affairs or community industrial relations or even to university presidents or chancellors.

In some cases, moves may be made back and forth between industry and academia, though it is somewhat more difficult to move from an academic environment into a corporate one than to go in the other direction. The abhorrent misrepresentation that "those who can, do, and those who can't, teach" is still in the minds of many career corporate senior managers. Given that many professors also run startup technology companies or extremely profitable consulting firms, there is absolutely no truth to that conception. Personally, I have come across highly qualified professionals in both industry and academia, as well as less than excellent people in both areas.

### Outlook

Since many computer professionals don't wish to obtain doctoral degrees and choose to pursue industry-based careers instead, there are usually a large number of openings at colleges and universities of all sizes. For example, the Association for Computing Machinery (ACM) monthly magazine always has at least four pages full of display ads for computer science, engineering, and information systems entry-level and tenured professorial positions. There is no reason to believe that a glut of professional university educators will occur in the computer field anytime in the near future, though funding constraints at many universities has begun to restrict the numbers of new openings more than some departments would like.

### Tip

Always strive to achieve a balance between academic prerequisites, such as paper publishing and research, and teaching. Almost everyone who has attended a major university has had professors who were far more interested in academic ladder climbing through prerequisite tasks unrelated to classroom instruction than actually teaching students. Most students are at a college or university to learn. Although the learning process is more than just classroom work, the material taught in a classroom and the outside student assistance that accompanies that instruction are essential to developing and graduating highly qualified professionals. There is a great deal of pressure at many universities to subjugate classroom work to other tasks; remember what your primary mission should be.

## Organizational Training Specialists and Managers

Some computer professionals enjoy the teaching and instruction process but don't wish to obtain a doctoral degree or work in an academic environment. They might consider a career path in the education and training field within vendors, corporations, or other types of organizations.

Every hardware and software vendor has an educational services (or similarly titled) department responsible for training customers, the firm's sales staff, customer support personnel, and others. As a training specialist, you would work with the development staffs and product managers to develop all necessary training courses as well as possibly teach some of the classes. For example, if you are a training specialist at a firm that develops and markets a word processing software package called ABCDEFWrite, you might develop a series of courses that includes:

- Introduction to ABCDEFWrite

- Advanced ABCDEFWrite

- Technical internals of ABCDEFWrite (for the customer support staff)

- Integrating ABCDEFWrite with desktop publishing packages, and so on

Even some large user organizations have training and education departments to conduct in-house training, though much of that has been slashed in recent years during corporate cutbacks and the training dollars are spent to send people to outside courses. The organizations that have maintained some amounts of training usually try to couple those responsibilities with development-type work on the part of their instructors.

Finally, many organizations, particularly those that develop commercial software with high sales volume, provide some form of computer-based training. The courseware is usually developed by the training specialists.

### Skills for success

Most of the skills applicable to university and college instructors we looked at in the preceding section are applicable to organizational trainers as well. Clearly written and verbal communications, technical insight, and a desire to help students are all-important.

### Educational background

Unlike university and college professors, a doctoral degree is not a prerequisite for success in the organizational education process. A strong technical background is still important, but since much of the training is product-specific, general technical knowledge is less important than knowing the ins and outs of the products for which courses are being prepared and taught.

### Career progression

Organizations usually have management hierarchies with various levels of educational services managers. Training specialists usually progress within these ranks. Some choose to move to an academic environment, and some of the more technically qualified professionals may move into a software development supervisory or managerial role.

### Outlook

The general climate of scaling back overhead has brought some pressure on educational service departments. Those who develop training that is for customer consumption—that is, customers pay to attend the classes—are more likely to escape cuts because they function as profit centers and earn real money for the organization. Those who develop training for internal organizations that are paid with corporate funny money (internal dollar transfers) are more susceptible to cutbacks. If you are interested in corporate training as a career you should, at least for the near future, try to attach yourself to an organization of the former type.

In addition, many seminar organizations such as Digital Consulting and Learning Tree conduct equivalent professional development courses. Those who wish to broaden their horizons and career options might try to become associated with one of those organizations.

**Tip**

Always try to find a satisfactory instruction level for each course you develop or teach. There will always be students who are more knowledgeable or are faster learners than others, and that leads to these *simultaneous* complaints: "This course was too hard." "This course was too easy and I didn't get anything out of it." You should make a very clear objective statement that includes the level of instruction in course descriptions and at the beginning of a course you are teaching. It is then up to the students to determine if your course is appropriate for them, and your course and instructor evaluations (and resulting career progress) are less likely to suffer unnecessarily from having a group of complaining, uninformed attendees.

## Finance and Investment Specialists

As most readers are aware, employment opportunities in the financial services industries have been on a downward spiral since the 1987 U.S. stock market crash. Since, as we saw in the Chap. 1, economic and environmental situations tend to be somewhat cyclical, computer professionals who have an interest in investments and finance might consider career options in an investment finance area such as one discussed below. The opportunities might not be there at present, but they will likely arise again at some future point.

The early and middle years of the 1980s saw tremendous growth in venture capital firms, mutual funds, and other financial institutions that specialized in investing in the computing industry. Since the best investment knowledge is a combination of raw numbers and knowledge about the area in which the investment is being made, opportunities were plentiful for those who not only had a strong investment finance background but also had knowledge about computer hardware, software, networks, and the other areas in which investments were being made.

### Skills for success and educational background

An optimum set of skills for when opportunities resurface is a background in computers and information systems coupled with a finance-oriented degree, preferably an MBA from a prestigious university. Whether you might be evaluating business plans and prospects for investment capital for a venture capital firm or analyzing software companies for a brokerage or mutual fund, a thorough understanding of the companies' underlying technical advantages and weaknesses as well as those of their competitors, is extremely valuable. This background will enable you to be able to look beyond the basic financial picture and help you to ascertain the target companies' potential for success and profits.

### Career progression and outlook

Once involved in the financial community, you might then diversify to any of a number of other specialties or move toward analyzing industries other than computer-related ones. Financial organizations have their own management structures, and progression along those ladders is possible. Again, the outlook is a little bleak now; but since the investment industry is cyclical and "money makes the world go around," it will likely improve over time. It may be some time, if ever, before the number of opportunities and accompanying compensations hit the levels found in the preceding decade, but this career could still be a good alternative for those who are tired of software development and the other direct positions discussed in this chapter but still wish to remain involved with the computer industry.

### Tip

If the investment finance area is one of your goals, prepare yourself now even though the current outlook is somewhat dismal. Obtain a graduate degree in finance and work on and learn from your own investments in the computer industry. You might try to obtain a lateral move into the corporate finance organization at your company. There are a lot of differences between corporate finance and investment finance, but there are also many overlaps, especially in asset and pension fund management. You might try to get involved in an investor services type of organization that manages 401K and company stock plans. The key is to be prepared for when opportunities become plentiful again, and you have some practical experience behind you.

## Computer Industry Recruiters

An alternative career path that would provide diversity of job functions yet allow you to remain involved in the computer industry is being a corporate recruiter—not-so-affectionately known as a headhunter. As a recruiter, your primary function would be matching the abilities of people looking for new positions with current and projected vacancies at client companies. Recruiters, especially those operating their own businesses, receive a percentage of the fees they earn for their companies, which in turn is usually a percentage of the salaries of those placed. In most circumstances, the client companies pay the fees to the recruiting firms; in others cases, the fees are client-paid. For those involved in the latter type of firm, it is expected that you would provide more than the initial screening of applicants and matching applicants with openings; if the job hunters are paying the fees, they usually expect in-depth interview coaching, résumé assistance, and other help with their job searches.

### Skills for success and educational background

Two of the most important qualifications a recruiter should possess are skill as an interviewer and insight. Interviewing skills are more than just asking someone about his or her career background or obtaining a list of job functions from a firm seeking to fill a staff position. In this particular career, success is predicated on *insight* into both client companies and job seekers. You must look beyond the printed words on a résumé and determine an applicant's true short- and long-term career goals, how well he or she really does know dBASE IV, for example, and possibly most important, whether he or she has a true record of success in completing tasks rather than just a list of projects started but never completed. You must also look at a company's requisition list and determine what type of person would be most suitable for open positions.

There really is no typical educational background for a computer industry recruiter. A business background with an emphasis on personnel management would be helpful but is not essential. A technical educational background also is helpful in being able to screen applicants with specialties in various skill areas. The Denver recruiting firm manager I interviewed for this book said that his recruiters and those of other firms with which he has been associated have widely varied educational backgrounds and that there is no correlation between educational programs and career success.

### Career progression

Some recruiters in larger firms may advance to office, district, or other management positions. An alternative is for recruiters to switch to or from corporate personnel management positions in the computer industry.

### Outlook

Given the employment and salary stagnation of the early 1990s, computer industry recruiting is a bit slower than it has been in the past. Although a number of people are being displaced from their jobs and utilize recruiting services to help find new positions, that is tempered by the smaller number of openings as well as the fact that those who aren't affected by downsizing are taking longer looks before they begin a job search. Often they choose to stay in a less-than-optimal position during the economic downturn.

A variation of corporate recruiting that has been active recently is outplacement services: Firms contract with major corporations who are conducting large-scale layoffs to assist the newly unemployed with their job searches. Outplacement services combine traditional recruiting functions with a heavier emphasis on résumé writing, interviewing skills, personal financial management (to ride out any unemployment periods), and career counseling.

## Tip

Honesty and integrity are very important when working with both job searchers and client companies. Some people have had unpleasant experiences with recruiters in the past, and those somewhat isolated incidents tend to sour the entire industry and give rise to the overstated notion of the greedy headhunter. The vast majority of recruiters with whom I have spoken or worked in the past have been no different from software developers, product managers, or other computer professionals in matters of integrity and ethics.

## Summary

This chapter has discussed most of the common computer industry positions in a number of different general areas from mainstream development and managerial career opportunities to such related positions as recruiter, investment specialist, and technical writer. There are a number of other job categories such as internationalization specialist (someone who is responsible for ensuring that products can be sold on the international market rather than just in the country in which they are developed) and the numerous semirelated positions such as production supervisor and graphic artist. The descriptions provided in this chapter are of the characteristics and backgrounds most typical for the mainstream types of careers. Again, responsibilities, job titles, and career opportunities vary widely from one organization to another. When searching for a new position, either at your current company or in the open job market, it is essential to analyze each opportunity with respect to the items discussed in this chapter: responsibilities, skills, background, career path, and general outlook.

## Career Success Profile: Michael W. Bray, Lead Systems Engineer, Martin-Marietta Astronautics

### Educational background

B.S., Computer Science, Louisiana State University, 1976

M.S., Computer Engineering, Air Force Institute of Technology, 1981

Graduate courses, Ada programming, University of Colorado at Colorado Springs

In-house corporate management courses at Martin-Marietta

### Career

U.S. Air Force computer officer, 1976–1984

Computer Technology Associates, 1984–1988

Martin-Marietta, 1988–present

Mike Bray supervises a group of 42 systems engineers developing a command and control system for the U.S. Air Force in Colorado Springs. Thanks to careful career planning, he has not only survived but prospered despite the many program cutbacks and resulting layoffs in the defense industry.

Originally an Air Force officer himself, Mr. Bray spent nearly 8 years on active duty before leaving the service to join Computer Technology Associates (CTA) in Colorado Springs in 1984. Though his last position in the Air Force had been as a branch chief managing 10 people, he took a position as an individual contributor with CTA without any supervisory responsibility. He worked on a series of requirements analysis efforts for the many systems the Air Force was procuring at that time for its Cheyenne Mountain warning centers, working his way back to supervising four people.

He saw an opportunity to join Martin-Marietta, a company involved in the same programs on which he worked at CTA, and again he became an individual contributor. Despite the conventional wisdom that moving from a supervisory or managerial role to a role without those responsibilities is a sure way to derail one's career, 6 months later he became a task order leader with 10 people reporting to him. Since that time, he has had a series of promotions to project manager positions, finally reaching his current level. Despite the technical-sounding job title of Lead Systems Engineer, Mr. Bray has more people reporting to him (42) than many people with the word "manager" in their job titles.

He spends a large portion of his time providing career advice and recommendations to his workers based on his 15 years in the computer and defense industries.

### Long-term career objectives

Remain in technical management roles.

### Best career move

Recognizing the match between opportunities at Martin-Marietta and his abilities and background and acting on that recognition.

### What he would change

Taking additional graduate university management courses at career points when the workload would have permitted it.

### Recommendations for others

**General.** "Software development is not the same as pure coding, but rather includes other portions of *systems* development. A successful software developer should understand all stimuli coming into a system, as well as all responses coming out of that system. A good software developer must have a systems engineering approach and know hardware, communications, and other components of the entire information system.

"I would recommend that an entry-level person get into a system engineering position first, rather than a job that requires only coding. That person can learn user needs and requirements and how to translate them into code requirements. Then he or she can learn the coding portions and, if that is the desired career objective, that person will be a better software developer for the time spent in the front end of the development cycle.

"Computer people should also stay up to date with new technologies, such as object-oriented design and communications. Even if they aren't directly applicable to their current jobs, they may be important in obtaining a new position, a promotion, or even holding onto current jobs in the face of cutbacks.

"They should also *write down* their career goals, and review them often. If they ever get to the point where the goals can't be met, they might want to consider whether they should move to a civilian-oriented industry or take some other career path. Each career move is a gamble, but they should try to factor in all the pros and cons. Sometimes you feel like a riverboat gambler and step outside your comfort zone into the unknown, but that is an important aspect of career planning."

**On the defense industry.** "The same things apply. Contractors are looking for well-rounded individuals, receptive to continuing education. People can't get into particular niches such as software testing and expect to stay there for the rest of their careers, given the current climate.

"People should keep an eye on current needs, as well as future directions. A good example is Ada. People knew what was coming and got involved in it, sometimes years before an actual development effort in Ada came along. When the opportunities came, they were ready, unlike the people who just figured they would learn Ada later."

**On technical management.** "A good technical manager must understand the 'people' component of system development, since they are as much an asset and an integral part of the entire system as the code and the hardware. The types and calibers of the developers must be understood, and matched to the tasks at hand."

### End Notes

1.  *Computerworld*, Oct. 15, 1990, p. 62.
2.  Alan R. Simon, *How to Be a Successful Computer Consultant*, 2d ed., McGraw-Hill, New York, 1990, pp. 6–7.
3.  Robert E. Kelley, *Consulting: The Complete Guide to a Profitable Career*, Scribner's, New York, 1981, pp. 15–16.

# 4

# Companies, Organizations, and Environments

Planning your career in the computer field is a far more complex function than simply choosing one or more of the positions discussed in the preceding chapter to pursue for current and future employment opportunities. You must now determine the type of organization on which to concentrate your search efforts.

There are major differences between, for example, a software development position at IBM and a similar position at the Internal Revenue Service. Even though the tasks, and the target hardware, may be nearly identical, there are differences in salaries, working environments, future career path opportunities, benefits, and even the methodologies by which the software is developed. This chapter will discuss the different organizational environmental factors and how they affect your present positions and future growth potential.

Figure 4.1 illustrates that, just as with software development (see Fig. 3.2), there is a multidimensional matrix with overlapping characteristics of organizational environments. On one axis is the type of organization. The distinction is more than just whether a firm is commercial (for profit) as opposed to not-for-profit; more important, it is whether the firm is a vendor or a user. Vendors, such as IBM and Oracle Systems, have environments that are oriented toward the primary assignment of developing hardware or software for resale to multitudes of customers, whereas a corporation such as USX or Texaco is primarily a consumer of computer technology: it uses hardware and software to accomplish its corporate mission. As we will see, there are also distinctions within these broad categories of vendors and users.

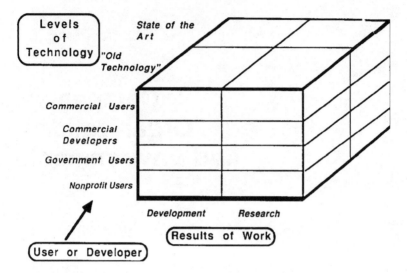

**Figure 4.1**  The organizational environment matrix.

The second axis is the goal of the computer hardware and software work being performed. Some organizations are oriented toward developing *production systems*—the systems used to perform real-life, often mission-critical, functions essential to operations. Others are research-driven; they work at the forefront of various technologies with goals of either predevelopment proof of concept, or in some cases, general discovery-oriented work. Note that specific job functions at a commercial vendor might be production-oriented (developing a product for commercial sale) and other functions at that same vendor might fall into a research category, such as testing new object-oriented technologies as a basis for development productivity. Of course, still other vendor functions, such as developing and maintaining the personnel and payroll systems for the organization, are in actuality user-oriented.

The third axis notes that organizations differ in the levels of technology with which they are involved. Some firms stay on the leading edge of all applicable hardware, software, and communications facilities, and others—for various reasons, which we will explore later in this chapter—tend to be risk-averse with respect to pursuing the incorporation of technological advances into their environments.

Finally, there is the concept of *organizational culture,* which pervades the other demarcations. There are many general types of organizational cultures, but each corporation, governmental organization, and not-for-profit firm tends to have its own, unique, dynamic culture.

As we will explore in this chapter, the three axes, plus the overall organizational culture, provide a large number of possibilities with respect to the organizational environment in which you might work. Just as matching your abilities and interests, along with environmental and other factors, with the specific job functions you perform is an important part of career success, and so is choosing an environment in which to perform those tasks and carry out those responsibilities.

## Types of Organizations

Figure 4.1 lists four primary classifications of computer organizations:

1. *Commercial users of systems.* These for-profit companies, varying in size from small neighborhood stores to multinational corporations, are primarily *users* of computer technology. That is, computer hardware and software is generally not a product of the company; instead, it is a tool to help accomplish the company's primary reason for existence: health care, automobile manufacturing, financial services, or any other of a myriad of applications. Computer systems are used to improve productivity, enhance profitability, and reduce expenditures. Some commercial users do try to market internally developed systems, with a mixture of success.

2. *Commercial vendors.* The products of these companies, and their primary reasons for existence, *are* computer hardware, software, complete systems, or services. Although these companies no doubt use computer technology in supportive ways similar to those adopted by the above-mentioned types of users, the primary reason for existence of these companies *is* the computer technology—the products themselves.

There are several different categories of vendors. Some fall into the grouping of hardware-oriented firms, those that traditionally have produced hardware and basic system software (compilers, operating systems) but not applications, tools, and utilities. Note that most of these firms, like IBM, Digital Equipment, and Hewlett-Packard, have in recent years striven to be providers of hardware, software, and services alike.

Other vendors produce no hardware at all, but instead develop software. These range from such firms as Oracle Systems, Informix, and WordPerfect Corporation that produce database management systems, CASE tools, word-processing packages, and similar software intended for wide audiences to companies that develop applications software for specific industries, such as construction or retail sales.

Still other firms are primarily service-oriented, as opposed to product-oriented ones like the hardware and software vendors just discussed, with services ranging from custom software development to general consulting. These include the consulting arms of the Big 6 accounting firms, system integrators such as the General Motors Electronic Data Systems division, and literally thousands of small software and consulting firms.

3. *Governmental users of systems.* These organizations are very similar to commercial users, the major distinction being that, except for revenue-collection agencies such as the Internal Revenue Service, state and local departments of revenue, and similar internal government organizations, they are not profit-driven. Computer systems are not developed and used to enhance profitability; instead, they are used to (hopefully) reduce expenses and improve productivity. Other than that, the major distinctions between governmental and commercial users are primarily in areas of compensation and working environments, as we will discuss later.

4. *Not-for-profit corporations.* These corporations represent a cross between commercial users and governmental organizations. They don't have a commercial profit motive (though they do use technology to enhance fund-raising activities), and unlike government organizations, they don't have a sometimes plentiful supply of tax dollars. Therefore, efficiency and effectiveness are arguably a more important criteria for computer professionals in a not-for-profit corporate environment than in a government one.

Computer opportunities and careers differ among these different types of organizations. Traditionally (though this has changed somewhat in recent years) informations systems and the people who staffed their development and use were considered a secondary, support staff function by all but commercial vendors. Even the most highly qualified vice president or director of information systems had little chance of reaching a company presidency or a corporate boardroom, because those positions were usually achieved through the line functions or sometimes the accounting and financial areas. On the contrary, since the business of computer vendors was and is exactly that—computer hardware, software, or services—software developers, hardware engineers, and most of those associated with developing the computer products are involved in the main function of the business rather than in support roles, and in theory they have career track potential to the highest levels of the organization. There are, of course, the same computer support functions—payroll, personnel, and so on—at computer vendors as at user-oriented firms, so don't mistake the above as stating that any software development manager at any vendor is on a career track toward the executive suite. As in user organizations, those who are involved in the line rather than staff functions and who can show direct profitability because of their computer-related efforts may have an edge in competition for various upper-level positions.

Even in the product line functions at vendors, there are distinctions to be made between the "main development" and the "support development," and they can affect the career paths of those involved in the various areas. For example, suppose a vendor is developing a database management system. The main development functions are those such as writing the language processors, memory and data storage managers, and the query compilers and executors. The people involved in these areas are at the center of the development effort, as opposed to the people who are developing the backup and recovery utilities, dump analyzers, portability tools, and metadata managers or are performing testing and quality assurance. That is not to say that salaries, promotions, bonuses, and follow-on positions will be radically and unequally different between those from these two subgroups, but the tendency is likely to be that given all things equal—meeting development schedules, achieving full functionality, and others—those at the center of the effort have a greater chance for financial and career rewards than those involved in the peripheral stages.

What does this mean to you and your career? It doesn't mean that you shouldn't get involved in development activities of a perceived peripheral nature; someone has to develop utilities and the unglamorous parts of products, and someone must assure product quality. It does mean, however, that you should, if you're involved in similar environments, watch very carefully how the rewards and recognition are distributed. If you have good supervisors and managers, they will recognize the importance of each and every area and make sure that the people involved are compensated accordingly. However, not all managers may think along these lines, and you owe it to your career path to ensure that you are not neglected in the reward and recognition area. You may point out how you joined a troubled, failing testing group and turned the success rate of that organization around, or you may become involved with product and system architectural efforts that provide greater visibility than if you were just sitting in your office or cubicle coding the backup and recovery routines.

Vendors tend to provide a bit more latitude *within the computer career field* to your career planning than do user organizations. As illustrated in Fig. 4.2, there are a number of follow-on positions available at a vendor that may not exist in a user-oriented environment. In a user organization, the latitude illustrated in Fig. 4.2 is not likely to be available unless you switch to a noncomputer job function or possibly move to a development-oriented subsidiary. Those career options are discussed in the next chapter.

Working in a user organization can sometimes be frustrating for computer professionals whose careers have revolved around technology and its implementations. Many people other than vendors, even high-

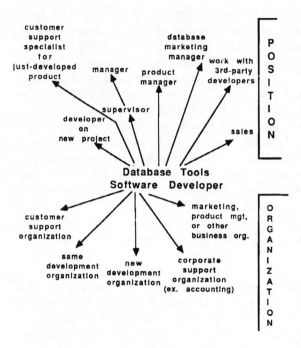

**Figure 4.2**   Vendor career paths.

level managers, may not be computer-literate or they have only somewhat brief experience with technology through personal computers and productivity software. Unless you can deal with people at a number of different levels, you may have problems, for example, explaining to a hospital chief of staff why the two summer interns he or she hired aren't likely to be able to develop a comprehensive image-based radiology management system over the next 6 weeks or implement a bedside network-based patient care system over the weekend. The higher your level of position in a user organization—corporate, government, or not-for-profit alike—the greater the value of your verbal, written, and interpersonal communications skills to job and career success. Many people in the computer field, as well as other professions, tend to be short-fused and frustrated, as well as cryptic, when attempting to explain technology and procedures to others outside the computer profession. Although you may be able to get away with arguing passionately over the actual megabits per second throughput after overhead on a thin-wire ethernet with another computer engineer, it is not advisable to pursue this course with a manufacturing manager for whom you are proposing a specific system solution.

Government organizations are, for the most part, very similar to corporate users. However, the differences appear in such factors as compensation (typically lower than in the private sector), job security (traditionally very good, but changing because of federal, state, and local budgetary problems in the past several years), and benefits (usually more vacation and holiday time than the private sector to try to make up for the lower pay and earlier retirement benefits than the private sector, especially in military organizations). The impression many have of government organizations is being chained to antiquated technology, but the past several years have seen great strides in hardware and software modernization at all levels of government, so that shouldn't be a factor in career planning. All in all, working in a large government organization is very similar to working for a *Fortune* 500 type of user organization.

There are also some unique opportunities available in government organizations that aren't available in the private sector. Some military computer officers might actually have battlefield responsibilities such as setting up forward computerized command posts. Those involved in the defense contracting sector of system developers may be involved in the hardware and software development, but the actual operation and hands-on work of these systems is likely to be left up to the military computer officers.

Another distinction between government organizations and private sector firms of all types is that the government groups usually are bound by very employee-protective rules and regulations. It is extremely rare to see people actually fired from government positions, except in cases of extreme nature. That is good in a way for purposes of job security as opposed to the massive corporate layoffs that have occurred in recent years, but it also makes it very difficult to get rid of poor performers. In recent years, there has been much discussion of layoffs of federal, state, and local employees in all areas, including computer-related job functions, because of cutbacks in revenue. Therefore, the job security that government workers at all levels have enjoyed to date may be affected in the future. Given that the (usually) lower compensation received by these workers than would be available in the private sector is often offset by such factors as job security, a new decision point must be factored into deciding to enter government service.

In the civilian—federal, state, or local—government side of this organizational picture, it is relatively easy if you desire to spend your entire career in one location. Military government members, of course, have to move fairly often, but not as often as in the past because of budget cutbacks. Whereas in the past a military computer officer would look at a change in location every 2 or 3 years, now the time between moves is closer to 4 to 6 years. Contrast that with corporate user and vendor firms, where promotions are often dictated by the willingness to move to new assignments. With the renewed international focus of many firms, overseas assignments are sometimes more common in corporations these days than for military members.

Direct salaries also tend to be lower than in corporate firms in other not-for-profit corporations, as well as in academic environments. However, as with government jobs, that is often offset by a higher level of benefits and indirect compensation. For example, a computer center manager at a university will probably earn a lower salary than someone in a similar position at a branch of a money center bank, but will likely have reduced or no tuition for courses taken at the university for him or her, as well as for his or her spouse and dependents. For someone with three or four college-age children, this could account for many thousands of dollars of indirect compensation.

## Development Goal

Another distinguishing characteristic among environments in which you may work is the goal of software or hardware development. Some organizations are *product-oriented;* that is, their primary goal is to produce a product for sale or a completed system to be run internally. Their products and systems must meet rigid standards in requirements conformance, error and problem handling, data integrity, performance, and many other areas. Other groups are primarily *research-oriented:* the products and systems being investigated are not, at least initially, for direct use by users or customers.

There are two primary types of research environments. One is oriented toward proof-of-concept, predevelopment work. An example might be using a prototyping tool to produce a screen-oriented prototype driver for user feedback before full-scale production begins. Another might be investigating various data-modeling techniques to determine which might be most effective in a database design CASE tool.

A second type of research work is oriented more toward investigative, exploratory work. The early days of RISC, neural networks, windowed graphics user interfaces, and object-oriented databases, when many projects were started at a number of organizations in each area, are but a few examples of investigative research that eventually moved into product realms. Universities are a primary location for investigative research, as are large corporations and government organizations where research-specific funds are allocated with an eye toward long- rather than short-term payback.

Careers and future growth can often take different paths depending on whether computer professionals concentrate on production or research environments. The optimal mix is to have backgrounds in both areas, particularly in the early days of your career. For example, spending 2 years doing production software development followed by another 2 years in a research-oriented department can provide progression possibilities into a supervisory opening in either type of environment in an organization. Employers—present and future—often like to see a mix of proven and forefront technologies in a candidate's background.

Someone who is very results-oriented and detail-driven might be most comfortable in a production development environment, whereas a professional who enjoys investigating new concepts but can't stand writing failover software and error-handling routines might be best suited to a position involving research. That distinction is true not only for developers, supervisors, and their managers but also for product managers, marketing managers, and others in various positions. A product or marketing manager who prefers a research environment might concentrate on forefront-of-technology development and give conceptual, high-level vision briefings to potential customers and at conferences, whereas a goals-oriented person considering one of those positions might be better suited to detailed product-specific presentations and work.

## Levels of Technology

Several mentions were made earlier about the levels of technology with which various positions are involved. A more detailed discussion is in the Organizational Culture section of this chapter, where you will find many of the reasons why some organizations seek out new technologies and experiment with their implementation whereas others avoid new software and hardware until absolutely necessary.

Most computer professionals prefer to work in a challenging environment that involves utilizing the latest in technology. There are, of course, those who don't wish to learn new programming languages, operating systems, and storage systems, but please heed these words of caution: *Involvement with state-of-the-art technology, as well as the lack thereof, is used as a cutoff factor in organizational downsizings, as well as the ability of those affected by the trends discussed in Chap. 2 to find new career positions.* If someone has been a software tester for the past 15 years testing maintenance code written in Jovial *and hasn't kept up with technological advances,* the odds increase dramatically, as time goes by, that the person will have a rocky career path ahead.

Aside from job security, involvement with new technologies often promotes career success by opening windows of opportunity. Chapter 9 discusses ways in which you can stay abreast of the many computer and communications technology advances even if your current position and tasks don't involve new languages, systems, and hardware.

Promotions and job offers are often influenced by the degree to which someone may, say, bring CASE technology into a company that has always designed software by hand. If you and another person are competing for a position and your background involves CASE, database, networks, and many of the other technologies discussed in Chap. 8 and the other person has little or no experience in those areas, you have a tremendous advantage even in nondevelopment positions. As long as you have the other skills and background desirable for that position, the exposure to and use of new technologies can often swing a job offer or promotion your way.

## Organizational Culture

Many readers are familiar with the term "corporate culture," which recognizes that corporations tend to have such societal characteristics as behavioral norms, levels of risk acceptance, and degrees to which rewards (income) are shared. Cultures apply to more than just corporations, though. That is why I prefer the term *organizational culture,* which indicates that government and not-for-profit organizations as well have cultures that affect the way they operate.

As with the other components of the corporate makeup we have explored in this chapter, organizational culture has a direct bearing on your career. We've already indirectly discussed one aspect of culture with respect to the levels of technology utilized at various firms, where some stay at the leading edge while others maintain outdated environments as long as possible. Some organizations tend to be very risk-averse; they hold back on implementing new technologies and techniques until they can no longer support their information systems environment with the equipment and software in place and must move ahead. Others look at leading edge technologies, such as CASE tools, object-oriented systems, and 4GLs as they appear and begin investigating how the technologies can may be integrated into everyday operations. The latter organizations aren't afraid to have failures and false starts.

The point is that the culture of the organization often dictates the level to which risks are undertaken. That applies to more than just whether new technologies are utilized. Risk-oriented firms will often go after the most difficult contracts and proposal efforts, try to develop hardware and software that "the experts" say will never work, try to open new worldwide markets, and generally provide a climate that rewards risk taking on the part of its members.

Risk-averse organizations, however, not only encourage maintenance of the status quo but sometimes even *punish* "unauthorized risk taking" within its ranks. Although that may seem ludicrous, the "punishment" tends not to be something so obvious as the CEO openly telling a risk-taking individual, "Don't do that again; we like things as they are around here." Rather, the risk-averse culture itself will usually find peers enforcing the norms. For example, suppose you are a software development manager and you, along with a forward-thinking product manager, try to bring to market a radically new CASE tool that utilizes new methodologies found to be promising in several university environments. If your organization is risk-averse, you are likely to gain initial verbal support for your efforts but run into one or more of the following:

1. The marketing manager questions your initial forecasts, indicating that he isn't sure a market exists for your product's new, unproven methodology.

2. The training manager explains that she just doesn't have the funds to develop customer and internal support classes in the current fiscal year because, you know, that last round of budget cuts...maybe next year the money will be there.

3. The customer support manager echoes the same sentiments of the training manager: "You know how things are this year."

4. Senior management cuts your previously approved number of personnel slots by one-third because of a slowdown in corporate earnings. You argue and argue that if you can reach your market window for the product, each person hired will be paid for 20 times over because of your projected returns on investment and payback period. They promise to study the idea further at the next staff meeting and get back to you.

And so on. The point is that the aversion to risk, or its acceptance, *directly* affects your job and responsibilities. You might be the most talented product manager or software development supervisor in the free world, but if you wind up in a company that not only doesn't reward successful risk taking but also has a culture which weeds it out and destroys it, your career is unlikely to benefit in any significant manner. And, readers, these cultures *do* exist.

Another aspect of organizational culture is the degree to which the rewards are shared throughout the organization. Some organizations, particularly for-profit ones, have environments in which earnings are widely distributed "to the masses" in the form of bonuses, profit sharing, and salary increases; others have little or no such distribution. Some of the former allocate the rewards based on *perceived* (and I stress that term) contributions to the well-being of the organization; others distribute on a more-or-less equal basis to all.

How does the reward concept affect your career? The first and most obvious way is the direct compensation you receive. Even though I stress throughout this book that there should be much more to career planning than just money, the simple fact is that unless you are already independently wealthy and are just pursuing a career in the computer career field so you don't have to spend all day watching soap operas and game shows, compensation *does* matter. It matters not only to your current standard of living but also to your career path; too many years at below-average compensation levels are likely to stagnate your future career growth either within your parent organization or if you decide to move to a new firm.

There is a motivating factor to the compensation as well. If everyone at the same job level, regardless of how well or how poorly they have performed, receives roughly the same salaries and additional compensation, the natural human tendency for all but the most highly driven people is to throttle back efforts and not put in those extra hours, and maybe start missing a deadline or two; the same raise and bonus will still be there, so why put in the extra effort? The inevitable result of this climate is that the fast burners, those most important to an organization's success, either leave or adapt their performance more toward the norm; either way, the organization's culture is likely to lead it into tough times.

Note that the preceding discussion is applicable not only to organizations that don't share their rewards with the employees but also to those that are generous but don't distinguish among the recipients' contributions before the sharing process. Human nature dictates that if you work twice as hard as and contribute twice the results of the person in the next office, receiving exactly the same bonus as that person will eventually affect your performance.

The converse also is true. There are some organizations that live by the motto, "What you did yesterday matters not the least bit; produce today or you're out." Some people actually thrive in such pressure cookers, but many people want the option to take an occasional vacation, maternity or paternity leave, or sabbatical or otherwise have some sort of a life outside their work environment. Burnout tends to be very high in those types of cultures, and the people who survive often experience eventual health problems and other debilitating effects. Obviously, the optimal culture is one that justly rewards efforts and results and allows refresh-and-regeneration periods. Those environments are somewhat few and far between; most cultures tend to fall toward one end or the other of the spectrum.

A final corollary in the monetary reward side of organizational cultures is the sometimes present inequity in regular and supplemental compensation. The trade and business publications often feature stories of founders and senior executives who steer a company into the ground through poor planning and management yet reward themselves with excessive salaries, bonuses, stock options, and golden parachutes while others who, at the worker level, are trying desperately to turn a company around are shut out of the reward picture and face layoffs or salary freezes and reductions. Needless to say, this also tends to affect performance of software developers, analysts, sales people, and those in other positions.

A nonmonetary aspect with respect to employee relations and culture is how people are viewed within the organization. Some firms view people as interchangeable parts, mere assets of the corporation; others tend to be more people-oriented and go out of their way to avoid layoffs, employee dissatisfaction, and other adverse effects on personal life. You should try to gauge employee turnover, how many employees get stranded in remote locations for months on end, and other factors that might give you an indication of your value to the firm as an individual.

Another aspect of corporate culture is the types of behavior norms to which you are encouraged to conform. Some norms are *relevant:* in order to belong to the organization, you must comply. An extreme example is that in order to be a software development officer in the U.S. Army, you can't be a member of the American Communist Party. A more realistic example is that if you will be a consultant to a Big 6 accounting firm, you will wear a tie to client meetings and behave in a very professional manner.

Peripheral norms are those which aren't "required" for membership to an organization but are important for further career success. If, for example, all the senior executives at a software firm are avid golfers with country club memberships, it would be advisable for someone wishing to make it into senior management at that firm to know the difference between a driver and a 9 iron. That doesn't mean that you have to be good enough to play in a pro-am tournament, but you should at least know a bit about golf, such as where the Masters' tournament is played every year. In another company, the "inner circle" might be filled with executives who raise horses on their farms or ranches, and someone desiring to fit in there should know the difference between, say, saddles used for western activities and those used for dressage.

The point is that, as with many other subjects discussed in this book, not a single one of these corporate culture topics has anything to do with how efficiently you may write a hash table procedure or your ability to use a CASE tool. Yet each and every one of these cultural topics is extremely important to career planning and success. The organizational culture should match your own career goals as closely as possible. If you hate golf and don't want to be on the fast track, avoid a software development position at a risk-seeking firm staffed by golf fanatics who are known to reward "their own kind." Instead, you might be more comfortable doing exactly the same development tasks in a government organization in which the staffers meet for beer and bowling every Wednesday and aren't frantically trying to keep their LANs at the leading edge of technology.

Two final notes about organizational cultures. First, subgroups within larger groups may have their own prevalent cultures that supersede those of the larger organizations. Many organizations have "black sheep" or "skunkworks" groups full of people who conform to an entirely different culture than the firm as a whole. The differences tend to be not in the relevant norms, but in the peripheral norms (see above). These people might be working on advanced research projects in a different location than the rest of the company. That a well-known corporation is famous for a particular environment doesn't mean that the organization you may join within that company will have the same culture. It pays to check.

Finally, organizational cultures are dynamic entities which change over time. People retire or move on and are replaced by others who may drive an organization toward a totally different set of standards and norms. Economic and other factors often drive even the most daring, innovative, and rewarding company into a defensive posture that requires layoffs of long-time employees. Don't expect that the culture in effect when you join an organization will remain that way forever. As with all of the factors discussed in Chap. 1, and with career planning in general, frequent investigation and appraisal of an organization's culture is recommended.

## Summary

Software development, hardware engineering, management, and nearly every other position discussed in the preceding chapter can vary widely in responsibilities and job functions, career growth potential, and compensation depending on the environment in which the tasks are performed. Every job environment should be looked at with respect to the characteristics illustrated in Fig. 4.1 and discussed in this chapter. I wish to emphasize once again that this does not necessarily mean that every single computer professional should be involved in fast-track, state-of-the-art, quick-paced corporate environments in which careers are made and broken on the basis of a single success or failure. Some people thrive in this type of environment; others, for any number of reasons, may prefer a different type of culture such as a university research laboratory, in which to work. *There is no "correct" or "incorrect" organizational environment;* instead, each person should, through the insight stressed throughout this book, determine which type of culture is best for him or her and strive to match that particular environment with a company or organization in which he or she will work. Remember that a major portion of your life is spent working in an organizational environment, whether it be your own, a *Fortune* 500 corporation, a small startup software company, or a software research laboratory. You should try to be as happy as possible with your choices, and don't be afraid to make appropriate changes as necessary.

### Career Success Profile: Marion (Skip) Pumfrey, Information Systems Consultant, Digital Equipment Corporation

#### Education background

B.S., U.S. Air Force Academy, 1967

M.S., Computer Science, University of Illinois, 1970

Air Command and Staff College, U.S. Air Force

#### Career

U.S. Air Force, 1967–1986

Air Commando Special Operations Intelligence Officer

Special operations in Vietnam

Information Systems Developer for Air Training Command

U.S. Air Force Academy Instructor

Manager, Strategic Air Command Intelligence Data Handling System (IDHS) Upgrade

Program Manager, Defense Intelligence Agency

Digital Equipment Corporation, 1987–present

Software Engineering Supervisor, Database Tools Group

Information Systems Consultant II, U.S. Service Delivery Services and Systems (SDSS)

Skip Pumfrey manages a group of 37 software developers at Digital Equipment Corporation that develops and supports all customer service call-management systems in the United States—25 systems in all. Skip spent 20 years as an Air Force officer following an enlisted stint and attendance at the Air Force Academy, retiring after 27 total years as a lieutenant colonel. Following several years as an air commando intelligence officer, he earned his master's degree in computer science at the University of Illinois, embarking on a long career in the computer profession. He developed training systems for the Air Force's Air Training Command and later returned to the Air Force Academy as an instructor. While instructing at the Academy, he also developed cadet evaluation systems and conducted research for the F-16 program office.

Skip's major accomplishment was managing and leading the successful development of the Strategic Air Command's upgraded intelligence-handling system, working 100-hour weeks for 5 straight years to bring in a badly understaffed and underfunded program. This tremendous effort is described below, and it provides a stunning example of successfully managing software and system development.

Following a final Air Force tour at the Defense Intelligence Agency, Skip retired from the Air Force and joined Digital Equipment Corporation. He spent several years in the database systems and tools area before joining the customer support organization to manage the development and integration of the call handling systems described above.

### Long-term career objectives

Remain in technical management roles.

### Best career move

Attending the University of Illinois through the Air Force, since it "was my entry into the computer field."

### What he would change

The last Air Force assignment at the Defense Intelligence Agency, since it was "devoid of technology, and I didn't produce anything; my 'value added' was to help program managers gain funding for their programs."

### Recommendations for others

**General.** "Invest a lot in staying current. Read avidly: not only topics directly related to your current jobs, but about other technologies as well. Also, conduct research to learn what others are doing, as you may be able to leverage off their successes and work to date.

"However, sometimes you have to 'put on the blinders' and focus on getting your product or system out the door. You should always try to make the effort to stay as up to date as possible, even when extremely pressured to complete your assignments.

"Good planning is key to project and program success. Plans should be extremely detailed and cover all possible contingencies, and you should manage toward your plan. Leadership is as important as management ability. You should not only have concepts and visions as to your short-term and long-term goals and objectives, but should be able to communicate them to others. You should also set an example; if long hours are required, you should be there with your troops. When times get tough, being right beside those working for you can sometimes be motivation enough to help them succeed in their tasks.

"Listening is very important also. You should listen to and learn from those working for you. Also, you must be able to sell your ideas to others over whom you have no direct authority. You must be persistent, especially if trying to foster change. It takes time and patience to generate and grow ideas.

"Organization is also very important. You must understand the work there is to do, as well as who you have—your resources—who can do that work.

"You must be able to adapt your management and leadership ability to your present situation. In the Air Force, I always tried to solicit input and participation from those working for me, but in cases of disagreement among various groups, a manager can always resort to 'pulling rank' to get all the players on the same page of the playbook. In a company such as Digital, which has an entirely different culture, everything must be negotiated among various groups. It is sometimes harder to reach agreements that satisfy peoples' different agendas, so the ability to sell your ideas is even more important."

**On hiring.** "Evidence of initiative and industry is critical. I look for those who have put forth the extra effort in the past, whether in school or at previous jobs. I also look to see if a person is a team player, and whether there is a good fit with the team already in place.

"Technical skills are important. Can the person contribute quickly? This doesn't necessarily mean that if I need a C programmer and the person doesn't know C but knows Pascal, Ada, Modula 2, and 10 other languages that the person won't be hired. If the person is a quick learner and has the evidence of initiative and is a team player, a small amount of technical training may be all that is needed to turn the person into a productive contributor quickly."

### A case study in program management

Chapter 3 discussed some of the success factors for software development supervisors and managers. A stellar example, one from which *every single reader of this book can learn,* is Skip Pumfrey's success in managing the implementation of the U.S. Air Force Strategic Air Command (SAC) Intelligence Data Handling System (IDHS) overhaul in the mid-1980s. Nearly 300 people—120 Air Force officers and 180 contractors—were led by Lt. Colonel Pumfrey's technical management of the entire program.

One of the keys, according to Skip, was a tremendous amount of up-front planning. Plans were developed and put into place quickly, and they were carefully followed up throughout the entire program. Another was rapid decision making throughout the entire program. SAC's leadership committed to decision making on the order of *weeks* because of the critical nature of the system. An automated project management tool provided reliable labor costs from the early stages which could be fed into the middle and latter phases of the program. At the end of the program, these cost estimates proved to be extremely ac-curate, and they were critical to the successful planning and manage-ment of the entire program.

Skip stayed heavily involved throughout the entire program, reading and reviewing each and every specification and document produced by each team, participating in most of the system design, as well as at-tending every single design review...a hands-on style he retains to this day in his work at Digital.

At the same time, Skip and several other senior officers were trying to institute better development methodologies and processes than cur-rently existed at SAC. They wrote entirely new development plans that detailed how to conduct reviews, tests, and all other steps of the devel-opment life cycle. Pilot projects in the overall program were set for any major changes to test the effectiveness of the effort. This entire "en-lightenment" effort took place outside the normal working hours, which really didn't matter since Skip worked about 100 hours nearly every single week for 5 straight years. Most of the officers worked 80 to 100 hours per week also, *and even the contractors kicked in efforts for which they didn't bill the government.* For anyone who has ever been in-volved in any form of government contracting, this simple fact is a tes-tament to the leadership ability and the examples set by Skip.

Throughout the entire program, Lt. Colonel Pumfrey "wandered around" to talk to nearly everyone on the development team. He would discuss the "big picture" and how their individual efforts fit into the success of the program and, more important, its critical mission. He conducted weekly reviews of schedules, variances, and all outstanding action items, seeking active resolution of any issues.

Another critical key to the program's success is that contingency planning was done from the very beginning. Contingency planning meant more to Skip than just listing possible risks; instead, it included detailed plans to overcome the problems with the highest likelihoods of occurring.

Testing was done very early in the development cycle. Since dedi-cated testers weren't provided for by the available funding, Skip did much of the testing himself. He found problems—not just specified fea-tures, but also performance, contention, and other systems-oriented discrepancies—early enough to permit them to be corrected before they propagated through the entire system.

One of the changes the program required was the move from a home-grown database management system to a commercial DBMS. They found early, due primarily to the testing efforts, that the commercial DBMS selected couldn't support the required number of concurrent users, and they were able to develop a multiple data manager scheme that ran on top of the main database and even performed some distributed update services that weren't available in most commercial database products of the time.

The end result was a critical, real-time, integrated system that was produced within budget and completed on time, *even though it was funded for only half as much as was required.* Most people in the computer field have had weeks in which they worked nearly nonstop; imagine putting 5 years worth of those together and leading a group of 300 people doing the same thing. Statistics indicate that most information systems development efforts either fail outright or are behind schedule and over budget. The development effort described here is one that doesn't fall to the norm, and its success is directly attributable to the hands-on, detail-driven, thorough management and leadership style demonstrated by Skip Pumfrey.

# 5

# Career Paths

In this chapter we will discuss some of the options, as well as the new challenges, facing you in the area of planning your career path. We'll look at traditional, straight-line career paths as well as cross-functional and dual-track career paths, along with a number of other topics that affect your career planning.

## Straight-Line Career Progression

The simplest career path on which to focus your efforts is a straight-line series of positions in relatively the same functional area. In Chap. 3, we mentioned that the traditional career path in many areas, particularly software development, was increasingly becoming an endangered entity primarily because of the turbulence and uncertainty in the computer industry. It is important, however, to understand this basic orientation to career progression, since all the variants we will look at shortly have their basis in this relatively straightforward model.

Figure 5.1 illustrates a typical straight-line career path. Note that the career progression over time shown here, from an entry-level individual contributor to a senior executive, is applicable to many of the functional areas we looked at in Chap. 3: software development, sales, customer support, and hardware engineering, among others.

Let's look at the software development in more detail with respect to this form of career path. An entry-level development position is likely to require minimal user contact and analysis work concentrating instead on rudimentary design and coding responsibilities. As someone in this type of position successfully completes a number of assigned tasks, he or she will then progress to functions that involve user interaction, a greater degree of analysis, specification, and design work, and possibly "chief programmer" or team leader responsibilities.

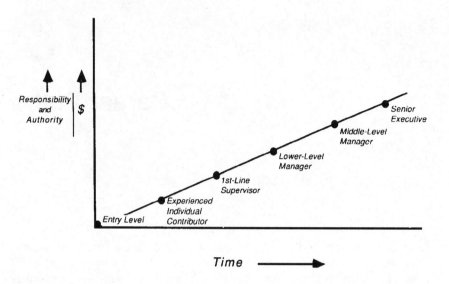

**Figure 5.1**   Straight-line career progression.

The next logical progression is to a first-line software development supervisor and then to a lower-level management position (see Chap. 3 for discussions about types of responsibilities). Promotions to middle management and, hopefully, the senior executive level are the natural progression.

Each major step is *usually* accompanied by increases in responsibility, authority, and compensation. More and more people are supervised or managed at each level, and there are increasing financial responsibilities in the form of budgets, profitability requirements (where applicable), and other components.

Note that this form of straight-line career progression does *not* necessarily occur at the same company or organization throughout your career. People often use one or more of the major milestones shown on the curve as points at which to decide whether or not to change organizational affiliations; in fact, points between milestones may also be used as points at which to decide whether or not to make a lateral move to another firm.

The major detriment to targeting a straight-line career path is that the path tends to level off well before the optimal goal of reaching the senior executive level. Given the number of factors we've discussed in this book, particularly those in Chap. 2, limiting your career to one functional area gives you *far less* flexibility than you might have if you were on a cross-functional career path (discussed next). If, for example, your entire career has been in the software development area and the environment is such as that of the early 1990s, in which development supervisors and lower-level managers often found their positions in jeopardy because of cutbacks, you have far fewer options with respect to preventive and defensive career actions than someone with skills in more than one area.

This is not to say that you should absolutely dismiss a straight-line career path from your planning. Instead, you should be aware of the potential pitfalls associated with such a targeted progression. If your goal is to progress through the software development ranks and remain in that area for your entire career, you should supplement your regular work with writing (books, papers, and articles), conference and seminar speaking, and other activities designed to give you a "presence" and make you stand out from the multitudes in the software development world.

## Cross-Functional Career Paths

A cross-functional career path looks, on the surface, nearly like its straight-line cousin as illustrated in Fig. 5.1, with one very important difference: the major milestones, as well as other points along the career curve, are often marked not only by changes in the job level but also by shifts in job functions. If you were following this form of career progression, you might begin as a hardware engineer specializing in peripheral devices, switch to writing software device drivers at the "experienced individual contributor" stage, and then advance to supervising the development of operating systems or database software. You might then move to a product management or marketing track as you advanced through the management ranks.

Following a cross-functional career path provides greater breadth in job functions than a straight-line track, but it usually doesn't permit you to become as technically familiar with each area in which you work. This type of career path is designed primarily for someone attempting to reach the executive suite in a mid-size or large corporation or in a government organization. The exposure to a number of areas throughout your career—and more important, a *successful* track record in each assignment at each level—can build a solid foundation from which you can draw to "make executive decisions."

The downside to this type of track is that because you may be switching job functions every 2 to 4 years, you need to cram as much knowledge and experience as possible into each of those positions to avoid becoming only superficially involved with each of the areas. Though each new job function is likely to involve a steeper learning curve than if you were progressing along the same functional track as sales or customer support, you must be able to function effectively as quickly as possible in each new assignment, *especially* in senior-level positions.

There are several secrets to aiding your learning process in this form of career progression. One is to have a well-defined, thoroughly thought-out career plan (discussed later in this chapter). Another is to work closely with those involved in the areas which are candidates for your next cross-functional career move. When I was an Air Force software development officer, I knew that when I left active duty I would probably initially work with a defense contractor, and I wanted to work in the bid-and-proposal rather than software area. I spent the last several years of my military time working with contracting officers on various system procurements learning the basics of the federal government procurement process. The knowledge gained helped me tremendously when I turned to the civilian world.

Similarly, after I had temporarily moved back into software development to obtain a position at a major computer vendor, I spent a great deal of my time assisting with product management functions, paving my way into a subsequent position in the latter area. Through actions such as these, you can ease your transition into new functional areas by being familiar with the tasks and responsibilities in those new roles.

## Dual Career Path Companies

One of the downfalls to both the straight-line and the cross-functional career tracks is that they force talented technical people who wish to progress throughout their careers—not just at the early stages—to phase down their technical activities and responsibilities in favor of supervisory and managerial activities *for which they might be poorly suited or which they have no desire to pursue.* We have already discussed that briefly in Chap. 3, noting that the computer profession, along with every other field, is full of technically talented people who have been kicked upstairs into supervisory positions in which they perform in a less than stellar manner. In most of these cases, the only way an organization could reward those people was to promote them into the next level of positions, which were supervisory in nature.

Several companies, including Digital Equipment (the one with which I am personally most familiar) have recognized this problem and instituted a dual career path system as shown in Fig. 5.2. Instead of a clear point at which technical positions evolve into supervisory and managerial ones, a split results in two tracks of *equal* pay, benefits, and status. One is the traditional supervisory and managerial path; the other is a continuation of the technical, hands-on types of positions in which computer careers usually begin.

The technical track positions usually evolve into such job titles as "consulting software (or hardware) engineer," "corporate consultant," and "senior corporate consultant." Instead of supervising the work and

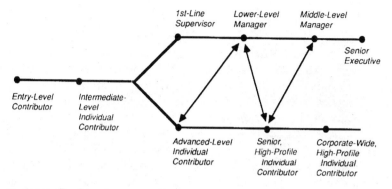

**Figure 5.2**  Dual-track career paths.

rating the performance of lower-level developers, these senior technical people may function as technical leads, senior designers, and internal consultants for major organizational programs such as developing
a new database management system or a new family of hardware platforms. They also function as organizational emissaries sitting on standards committees and giving presentations to key customers and
clients.

The important feature of this dual set of career paths is that it recognizes that some people have no desire to become managers, wear
suits, or otherwise conform to the norms of "business positions." Yet
there should be some way to reward these types of professionals
through promotions and salary increases, since they may be valuable
contributors the organization doesn't wish to lose.

There are usually opportunities to move back and forth between the
two tracks. It is far easier for someone to move from the managerial
track to the technical one than in the other direction—particularly at
the uppermost levels—though there are many cases in dual-track companies in which this does occur.

Someone following the technical side of the dual-track career path is
less likely to rise to a chief executive officer or chief operating officer position than someone from the managerial side. Usually, however, this
isn't a career aspiration of people on the technical side, since they are
on that track primarily because they don't wish to have responsibility
for managing people and budgets and prefer instead to focus their talents on technology.

Finally, following a technical track in this type of organization is usually an alternative to pursuing a research-intensive academic career or
operating a solo consulting firm. For those whose primary goal is to remain at the forefront of technology and have the assets and support of
a large corporation behind them, it would be worthwhile to investigate
companies that offer this type of career environment.

## Career Planning

Successful careers *usually* do not happen by accident. That does not mean that each career move is preplanned and cast in stone; we've been stressing flexibility and versatility in the face of rapid changes in the many different areas we've discussed. There should be, however, a "master plan" that you frequently review, revise as necessary, and in general use as the blueprint to your career.

A career plan should, for these purposes, be a written document that you keep with your other important papers. Figure 5.3 illustrates a sample career plan. There will invariably be more uncertainty and less precision in the latter years of your plan, but you should have some general idea of where your odyssey through the computer world is intended to lead you.

Such factors as your primary job function, the industries in which you work, educational goals, target compensation, and general objectives should be documented. As I've mentioned previously and discuss later in this book, changes in family and other personal situations often lead to revisions along the way. Your goal at age 21, for example, might be to be CEO of IBM or AT&T. At age 30, it may have changed to starting and building your own software company, and at age 40 it might now be to run a one- or two-person consulting firm. *There is neither crime nor shame in recognizing your changing personal and professional needs over time.* That is much better than clinging to outdated objectives. Just because you told your fraternity brothers or sorority

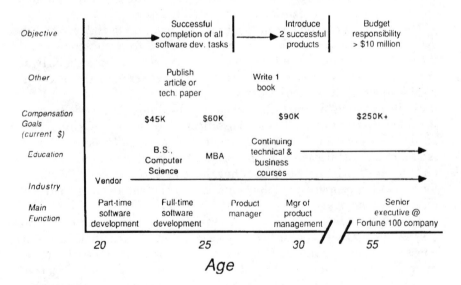

**Figure 5.3**  Sample career plan.

sisters that you would be worth $10 million when you hit age 30 or would retire at age 35 doesn't mean that you set an unalterable goal.

Your career plan should be reviewed frequently—at least annually—and you should:

1. *Update* all applicable portions to reflect changing goals or situations, including environmental changes and the types of personal changes which we've just discussed.

2. *Review* your updated plan with respect to the current realities of your career.

3. Determine if *corrective action* (e.g., pursuing a change in employment) is required.

By making planning and review an important and regular part of your overall career management strategy, you can assist your progression throughout your entire professional life.

## Taking a Step Backward

One of the rules of conventional wisdom with respect to career planning has always been to avoid, whenever possible, "backward movement" in your career path. That is, if you are a software development supervisor, you shouldn't ever become an individual contributor, because that implies to the world that you not only weren't able to progress in your career but weren't able to handle the tasks to which you were assigned.

First, read the Career Success Profiles of both Skip Pumfrey (Chap. 4) and Mike Bray (Chap. 3). Both men have made career moves that some would term "steps backward" by supervising a smaller number of people or moving to a technical position from a supervisory one. Note, however, that both of these successful managers quickly "recovered" and now have even greater responsibilities than they have had in the past. In neither case would I consider their career paths derailed by the shifts they have made. In fact, moves today to new companies often require a 6-month or so "breaking in" period before additional managerial responsibilities are given to individuals. Both of the professionals, as well as countless others in the computer field, are proof that solid career planning can overcome such situations as switching back and forth between supervisory and technical roles. In fact, that is the basis of the dual-path career option we discussed previously.

Second, the economic environments today often require, say, a manager of customer support to move to a hands-on technical support position in the face of corporate cost-cutting. Since it isn't quite as easy today to resign and quickly obtain a new job at another company as it was a few years ago, many professionals find themselves forced into situations in which in order to retain employment they must make what others would consider a step backward in their career.

As with longer periods of unemployment, there is less of a stigma today attached to a backward career move than there once was. In fact, some managers might look at someone who was willing to make the tough move and absorb the sacrifices as a survivor, as someone who is willing to do what is best for his or her career as well as the organization as a whole.

The point of all of this is that, given the climate in the computer profession today, many more people than ever before may be required to consider career moves that are neither lateral nor promotional in nature. Rather than dismiss such moves outright, you should take all of the factors discussed in this chapter and the book into consideration.

## Auxiliary Work in Your Career Path

One of the ways in which to promote your career is to use auxiliary, outside work to overcome shortcomings in your past or present positions. We've looked at how an Air Force pilot was able to keep up to date with LAN and other technology (Chap. 2's Career Success Profile) and, also in Chap. 2, discussed moonlighting and outside work as preventive actions in these turbulent times. Such measures should be an integral part of your written, documented career plan that we discussed earlier in this chapter.

## Your Own Company in Your Career Path

Along with considerations of auxiliary work, your career plan should include aspirations for starting your own company—software development, consulting, technical writing, or another type of business—as well as the preparatory actions you must take. If, for example, you plan to gain 3 or 4 years of database and CASE experience at your present company and then start your own consulting firm, your career plan should also include preparatory steps including:

- Writing and speaking on these technologies
- Doing outside, supplemental work
- All of the preparatory steps necessary to start your own company[1]

Through constant attention to these preparatory and auxiliary steps as part of your overall career strategy, you can increase the chances for success in that venture. There are times, however, when you may find yourself going out on your own as a reactionary rather than planned step. If you find yourself suddenly without full-time employment (see

Chap. 2), you may wish to consider starting a consulting or other service company. It is, of course, preferable to have planned to go out on your own in order to take the many preparatory steps discussed earlier in this section. In the unplanned situation, however, you may be forced to revise your career plan in order to account for the new set of conditions that require solo operations.

## Getting Ahead in the Computer World: A Career Perspective

There isn't a magical checklist of actions and steps that you can follow to succeed in the computer career field. All the subjects approached in this book are very important in achieving career success. From a career path perspective, however, there are several items that bear consideration with respect to your career planning:

1. You should have a *demonstrated record of accomplishments.* Employers and hiring managers want to see more than broad experience with technology and other career skills; they want to see success and accomplishment in those positions.

2. You should strive to have *budgetary and profit center responsibilities.* In order to progress through corporate, and even government, organizations, you must be able to handle budgets and, preferably, know how to achieve required returns on investments in the assets under your control.

3. You should have *foresight* with respect to technology. Chapter 9 discusses ways to keep on top of technological advances, and Chap. 8 discusses some of the most lucrative technical areas for the 1990s.

4. You should, over time, show an *increasing level of responsibilities.* That doesn't preclude taking an occasional step sideward or even backward in order to further your career, but such moves should lead to even greater responsibilities in the not-too-distant future.

5. You should understand the nature of *organizational politics.* As we discussed in Chaps. 3 and 4, politics and conformance to corporate culture norms are often as important, if not more important, than technical and managerial abilities in receiving promotions, bonuses, and other rewards.

By keeping the above items in mind when planning career moves, you can help to increase your chances for overall career success.

## Summary

This chapter has focused on tying together many of the individual items discussed in the first four chapters into a comprehensive, flexible career plan. Focusing on such a plan is critical for your career success.

You should have some idea of what your short- and long-term objectives are, as well as the steps necessary to achieve those goals.

## Career Success Profile: Donald M. Jacobs, President, Inteck, Inc.

### Education background

B.A., Astronomy Mathematics, UCLA, 1962

M.S.A., George Washington University, 1970

C.P.A., C.D.P.

Numerous professional and continuing education courses

### Career

Jet Propulsion Laboratories, 1962–1966

Bendix Field Engineering, 1966–1972

Massachusetts Hospital Association, 1972–1974

Illinois Hospital Association, 1974–1976

Samaritan Health Systems, 1976

Pannell Kerr Forster, 1977–1982

Inteck, 1982–present

Donald Jacobs is cofounder and president of Inteck, Inc., one of the leading consulting firms specializing in hospital information systems. His long career in the computer field began in the early days of the space program; he worked as a scientist at the Jet Propulsion Laboratories developing software for orbital mechanics for the flight plan analysis group. He worked on the Mariner II (the first unmanned flight to Venus), Surveyor, lunar orbiter, and Mariner IV (the first unmanned flight to Mars) missions developing a wide range of software from TV camera management to trajectory systems. He also completed work in 1964 for the solar system "grand tour" which was launched in the late 1980s. He moved to Bendix Field Engineering, initially to support the Goddard Space Center and the manned space program, bringing with him much of the software he had developed at JPL. He moved into supervisory and management positions, eventually managing a group of 18 people providing trajectory analysis for the lunar program.

Following his space system days, he formed a group at Bendix that provided custom software development and consulting services for outside clients, eventually rising to a department manager position. In 1971, he received a contract at a Chicago hospital to develop a rule-based expert system for kidney stone prediction and treatment. Early test cases showed a 30 out of 33 case agreement with attending physicians; upon further review of the cases with differing diagnoses, each showed the physician had missed various symptoms and data points and the expert system was indeed correct. This system became the basis for all kidney stone patients at the hospital, and it provided Don with his first exposure to health care systems, a career path which he would then pursue for the balance of his career.

Don joined the Massachusetts Hospital Association as the director of research and development, responsible for looking years down the road to predict and address the information systems needs of hospitals. He developed a Definition of a Hospital-Based Industry Information System which was an early conceptual model for hospitals to adopt.

Don joined the Illinois Hospital Association in 1974 as the vice president of program development, specializing in shared service programs among various subgroups of hospitals in Illinois. He was instrumental in negotiating a standardized contract for 52 hospitals with a major health care systems vendor, providing cost relief to a number of hospitals in Illinois.

He then joined the Samaritan Health Systems chain as the corporate director of MIS for a brief period, and later became a free-lance consultant, one role of which was being the executive director for the American Association of Health Data Systems (AAHDS). Through a contact, he then joined Harris Kerr Forster, a national public accounting firm, as the first national director of computer services. He specialized in the hotel and hospital industries (two very similar industries with respect to operations), wrote a column for a monthly newsletter, and earned his CPA. He became a principal of the firm and later a partner of the now-titled Pannell Kerr Forster (after several international mergers).

Don left to found Inteck in 1982, eventually specializing in the firm's operations in hospital systems. Inteck developed several commercial packages including a radiology management system which was marketed by Burroughs as part of its product line. Inteck had several computer systems agreements with other firms such as Konika, and for a time it had too much business, which almost was detrimental to its operations. In 1987, Inteck joined a company in New York as the Inteck Division. In 1989, Don bought back the consulting portion and the rights to use the name "Inteck." Since then, the firm has been extremely profitable, with revenues and profits increasing each year as its presence in the health care industry continues.

### Best career move

Moving to the Massachusetts Hospital Association, which brought him in contact with the health care industry. He was able to merge his computer technology background with the needs of an industry in its infancy with respect to automation.

### What he would change

"I really haven't had any misstarts; all of the moves have worked out rather well."

### Recommendations for others

**General.** "People often try to do what they may not be able to do well, almost as a measure of defiance. One of the keys to career success is to understand your own strengths and weaknesses and to work with people who are strong in the areas in which you are weak. There is a great deal of synergy in a successful organization. If you detest detail work but are very good at large-scale, strategic planning, become associated with or hire someone who is a very good detail-oriented person.

"Sometimes working for yourself can be best; at other times the complementary skills (discussed above) with others are what may be best.

"It's OK to be happy with what you're doing. There are a number of industries in which you can apply your computer, or other, knowledge and experience. If you are getting burned out on a specific industry, change to something you enjoy. Don't get caught in a rut. You *can* learn new industries and technologies." [Author's note: Don Jacobs is a prime example of this, moving from the early days of the space program to hospital systems to public accounting, and being successful in all three areas.]

**On consulting.** "You should always give it your best shot for clients. Understand that clients don't always accept your recommendations, for a variety of reasons, but you shouldn't take this personally. You have to be able to handle this conflict, or you will have problems in consulting. As long as you do your best work, are objective, and present your findings as clearly as possible, you have done your job. Your client is usually the ultimate decision maker, and you have to realize that there are a lot of other factors involved aside from technology and financials, such as political climates and organizational cultures."

### End Note

1. See Chaps. 1 to 6 of Alan R. Simon, *How to Be a Successful Computer Consultant*, 2d ed., McGraw-Hill, New York, 1990.

# Chapter 6

# A Guide Through the Computer Education Maze

As an illustration of how important it is for *you* to choose an educational program that is the most beneficial for you and your career, let me begin this chapter by telling you how I accidentally chose my particular computer-oriented undergraduate degree program over 15 years ago. Even if you are already a professional in the computer field, you may be contemplating a graduate degree or other continuing education. This chapter is *especially* important for any reader who is considering entering the computer profession as a first career and is planning his or her initial education and for others considering their professions in this field. As was mentioned in Chap. 1, education and training are key components in the computer career success picture, and there are a number of factors that should be considered in choosing both initial computer education and continuing education.

Back in early 1976, I received an Air Force Reserve Officer's Training Corps (ROTC) scholarship that required my choosing a college undergraduate major from an approved list of scientific, engineering, and technical programs. The only degree that looked even remotely interesting to me was that of computer science. I knew absolutely nothing about computers, but I had just received a Texas Instruments calculator as a gift and figured there had to be some relationship there. Besides, computer science seemed more interesting to me than physics, chemistry, mechanical engineering, or aeronautical technology.

I applied to the computer science department at Arizona State University in Tempe, which was where I had decided to attend college. When I had been accepted, I was horrified to find that the acceptance package contained a description of the required prerequisite and corequisite classes for a computer science degree, such as wave phenomena, heat mechanics, fluid dynamics, calculus IV, and all sorts of other classes that looked extremely foreboding to me. Just when I assumed I was guaranteed to flunk out before my first year was completed, I discovered that the College of Business Administration at ASU had a degree program in computer information systems (CIS), which had required courses like marketing, accounting, statistics, and business (e.g., easy) calculus. This was the program for me! I was able to get the Air Force to allow me to major in CIS as a technical subject, even though it was in the business college, because the Air Force was very short of computer officers at the time, and anyone with any form of computer education was needed.

What is the lesson here? Simply this: all "computer" education degree programs and majors are *not* the same. To this day, I still talk to high school students considering a career in some aspect of information systems and to people considering switching their profession into the computer field. Most state that they plan to major in "computers," and they are surprised to find that there are vast differences between, for example, a computer science major and a program in business-oriented information systems. To complicate matters, not all programs that carry the same title are equivalent. Some computer science programs, particularly those in colleges of engineering, might emphasize hardware and circuit design and be more like a computer engineering program, whereas others might have a strong emphasis on systems programming topics such as compilers, operating systems, and language theory. Still others are very mathematically oriented, yet some may look very much like a business information systems program.

We will explore the various types of curricula, emphasizing the decision-making process in matching an education program with *your* interests and aptitudes. The personal experience related in the preceding paragraphs is intended to emphasize that in my particular case I don't think I would have been nearly as comfortable in a computer science or computer engineering program as I was in a business major. More important than the relative degree of difficulty in the type of degree program itself is the direct bearing on career success, or lack thereof. *This chapter is intended to ensure that you don't have to get lucky and "accidentally" choose an appropriate undergraduate or postgraduate education program.*

## The Computer Majors: What Are They?

### Business-oriented information systems

These programs are mostly found in colleges of business administration, and they are usually entitled Computer Information Systems (CIS), Management Information Systems (MIS), or sometimes just Information Systems (IS).

When I was pursuing my undergraduate degree in CIS at Arizona State University in the late 1970s, that degree program, as well as most other IS-type majors, was heavily oriented toward COBOL programming and structured design, with collateral emphasis on database management systems and accounting information systems. Since that time, most IS programs have expanded their scopes to cover other prevalent computer subjects.

Let's look at a representative undergraduate IS program, the Bachelor of Science degree in CIS at King's College in Wilkes-Barre, Pennsylvania. The course sequence requirements are shown in Table 6.1.[1]

Several things are significant about this particular program. First, there is an emphasis on a variety of computer subjects applicable to the "real world." The sophomore year course in COBOL/CICS programming is a recognition that real-life software development doesn't rely solely on programming languages such as COBOL and FORTRAN; rather often, it includes such software systems as transaction processing monitors. The ability to learn CICS programming as an undergraduate can be very valuable to graduates of this program and give them an edge in the competition for positions that utilize IBM mainframe technology products such as CICS. Other courses available as electives can help students learn RPG II, Basic, and other languages deemed necessary to meet one's educational goals.

Second, a course in C is required. Although the C language is often thought of as a computer science language rather than a business programming language, the fact is that more and more positions today re-

**TABLE 6.1  Undergraduate CIS Curriculum**

| Year | Fall semester | Spring semester |
|---|---|---|
| Freshman | Principles of Accounting I<br>Computer Systems and Information Flow | Principles of Accounting II<br>Introductory COBOL<br>  Programming |
| Sophomore | Intermediate COBOL Programming<br>Macroeconomics | Advanced COBOL/CICS<br>  Programming<br>Managerial Accounting<br>Statistics course |
| Junior | Systems Analysis, Design, and<br>  Implementation I<br>C Programming<br>Database Management Systems<br>Business elective | Systems Analysis, Design,<br>  and Implementation II<br>Advanced Microcomputer<br>  Concepts |
| Senior | Applied Software Development Project<br>  or Internship<br>Management of Computer-Based<br>  Information Systems | Data Communications<br>CIS elective |

quire the knowledge of C, Ada, or other "software engineering" languages, which is how C can really be classified. The knowledge of C can give the graduate of this program an edge over an IS graduate from another institution who hasn't had the opportunity to be exposed to such a widespread programming language.

Third, a required course in microcomputer concepts ensures that the program's graduates have a multilevel mentality with respect to computer technology rather than just a mainframe, batch-oriented framework.

Finally, note the sprinkling of business courses such as macroeconomics, accounting, and statistics. Some programs, such as Arizona State's when I was there, included such business courses as marketing and finance; having some basic business understanding is important for any CIS major.

Graduate IS programs are similar in concept to those at the undergraduate level. There tends to be a mix of business and computer topics, with some programs being more technically oriented than others. One very technical program is at the University of Arizona, rated one of the top ten IS programs in the United States (see Program Rankings section below). Arizona requires preparatory work in finite mathematics, statistics, economics, business law, accounting, finance marketing, organizational behavior, production, and business policy—quite a load of business courses.[2]

The computer courses include topics in:[3]

- Computer graphics
- Computer-aided information systems analysis and design
- Data structures and database management
- Design and control of production systems
- Material requirements planning (MRP)
- Artificial intelligence and expert systems
- Domestic and international issues
- Soviet technology and science
- A variety of computer mathematics courses, such as stochastic models, multivariate analysis, and discrete mathematical programming

Note the difference between this program and the undergraduate CIS program at King's College (Table 6.1). Aside from the obvious difference that one is at the undergraduate level and the other is at the master and doctoral levels, you can see an entirely different emphasis in the subject courses. There are courses in systems analysis and design, for example, in both programs, but the real-world courses are very different at the two schools. Someone combining an undergraduate degree from King's with a graduate degree from Arizona would run little risk of duplicating course loads at the undergraduate and graduate levels and thus would gain a broad educational and practical background from both programs, even though both are in the IS area. *This is very important to look at when choosing graduate education: that the program complements, rather than duplicates, your undergraduate work.*

### Computer science

Table 6.2 illustrates a typical computer science undergraduate program at King's College, which you should compare with the undergraduate CIS program of Table 6.1. You will note several important differences between the two, and they are representative of the distinctions between IS and computer science programs. First, the computer science program has a heavier emphasis on required mathematics than the CIS program. That is primarily because computer science courses tend to be more algorithm-intensive than their IS counterparts, even when the courses have similar titles. For example, a computer science data structures class is likely to emphasize the mathematics behind the various tree structures and sorting algorithms, whereas an IS data structures course will probably concentrate more on, "This is a linked list; this is a B*-tree; here's how they are used in commercial DBMS products." The mathematical foundation is helpful for computer science students to fully understand the algorithmic

**TABLE 6.2    Undergraduate Computer Science Curriculum**

| Year | Fall semester | Spring semester |
|------|---------------|-----------------|
| Freshman | Computer Systems and Information Flow<br>Foundations of Math<br>Analytical Geometry and Calculus I | Introduction to COBOL Programming<br>Problem Solving and Programming in Pascal<br>Computer Design and Architecture<br>Analytical Geometry and Calculus II |
| Sophomore | Problem Solving and Programming in PL/I<br>Discrete Mathematics<br>Analytical Geometry and Calculus III | Data Structures<br>Microprocessors<br>Linear Algebra |
| Junior | Computer Graphics<br>Assembler Programming | Operating Systems<br>Modeling and Simulation |
| Senior | Software Engineering | CS elective* |

*Elective chosen from Artificial Intelligence, Programming Languages, Systems Optimization, Numerical Analysis, or Compilers.

nature of many of their courses. This is obviously not a firm distinction, since the graduate MIS program at the University of Arizona has many mathematics-oriented courses, though they are elective rather than required.

Second, note the computer science emphasis on compilers, operating systems, and related topics as opposed to the IS applications analysis and design orientation. That is primarily due to the "old days" when computer science graduates were likely to become systems programmers and IS graduates entered the applications world. As the distinctions blur, you see more course crossover such as COBOL—traditionally a business programming language—being a required computer science course in King's computer science department.

Graduate computer science programs are similar to their undergraduate counterparts in content type, except that some offer much more detail in the theory and practical internals of hardware and software. Stanford University typically has one of the "top three" computer science programs, along with M.I.T. and Carnegie-Mellon University. A look at the Stanford catalog reveals one of the most comprehensive computer science programs found anywhere.[4] Six different concentration options are available to computer science graduate students, including:

- Numerical analysis/scientific computation
- Systems
- Software theory
- Theoretical computer science
- Symbolic and heuristic computation
- Database

In addition, a detailed program of core courses is required of all enrollees regardless of their area of concentration. From reading the course requirements, both general and by concentration, it looks as though an expert system is required to understand the possible combinations of the many available classes; it's no wonder that Stanford's computer science graduates are so highly thought of in the computer world.

The concentration areas available at Stanford illustrate what I have referred to several times before: that the title "computer science" can denote a wide variety of possibilities in available courses. A program like Stanford's includes the six areas of emphasis listed above, so an enrollee may concentrate in any one of the practical or theoretical areas available. Most universities and colleges don't have as comprehensive a program, which is why, prior to enrollment, it is *critical* to investigate whether, for example, your prospective program emphasizes numerical analysis and scientific computation, symbolic and heuristic computation, or another course orientation. For those who may not be oriented toward theoretical topics, "accidental" enrollment in a program for which your aptitudes might not be strongest can lead to major career setbacks and false starts.

To illustrate how programs are often different from one another, let's look at Pennsylvania State University's computer science program.[5] Courses are taught in operating systems, data structures, and compilers as at Stanford and King's College, but Penn State's program also includes courses in computer applications in chemistry, advanced programming and job control language, and other courses unique to this particular curriculum. Since academic programs change over time along with changes in technology, it is important when investigating undergraduate or graduate programs to always look at the most recent catalogs, as well as talk to department faculty members to determine any "special topics" courses or upcoming additions to or deletions from their programs.

### Artificial intelligence

Many computer science and IS programs, including those described above, have courses in artificial intelligence (AI) and expert systems. Several universities, most notably Stanford, M.I.T., and Carnegie-Mellon University—the same three schools considered among the top of the computer science education world—have especially strong programs in the artificial intelligence area.

AI programs emphasize the same types of courses as "regular" computer science degrees, but the courses are oriented toward AI and expert system technology. For example, programming languages are likely to teach Lisp and Prolog in addition to or instead of FORTRAN and C. Database courses are oriented toward object-oriented databases and knowledge bases. Systems analysis and design courses are usually supplemented by or replaced with subjects in knowledge engineering and knowledge representation. Just as King's College's CIS program had a course that teaches "real-world software development" using CICS, a top-notch AI program will have a course that features software development using an expert systems shell to create forward- or backward-chaining expert systems.

### Computer engineering

Many universities have computer engineering programs that are separate from yet related to the electrical and mechanical engineering degrees. Those wishing to enter the hardware design and development world might consider a computer engineering degree at the undergraduate or graduate level in conjunction with a computer science degree at the other. Computer engineering programs are oriented toward circuit design, physical data communications media, and other hardware-intensive topics.

Penn State's computer engineering program, for example, contains courses in:[6]

- Computer systems architecture
- Digital integrated circuits
- VLSI circuits
- Electronic analog computers
- Introduction to hybrid computation

These courses, coupled with instruction in operating systems, input-output architectures, and other highly technical systems-oriented subjects, provide graduates with the foundation on which they can build hardware-oriented careers.

### Specialized programs

In addition to the programs in artificial intelligence described above, some universities and colleges have other forms of specialized computer degree programs. Two examples are Stanford University's medical information sciences (Med IS, to distinguish it from our use of MIS to mean management information systems) program and Purdue University's computer-integrated manufacturing technology (CIMT) degree.

The Med IS program at Stanford is for computer professionals, as well as physicians and others in the medical field, who wish to combine computer technology with medical applications and requirements. Many of the degree courses are identical to those taught in Stanford's computer science program, but they also include topics in clinical diagnosis, introduction to clinical environments, computer-assisted medical decision making, and computer applications in medicine.[7] This program—whether taken at the master's, doctoral, or post-doctoral levels (three different degree programs are available) provides the basis from which a career in medical and health care information systems can be launched. Although general computer science and IS topics are also valuable toward a medical systems career, the unique, specialized training available is likely to give a Stanford Med IS graduate a tremendous edge in his or her area of specialization.

Similar "career jump starts" are possible in the computer-integrated manufacturing (CIM) area through Purdue University's degree program. According to Purdue's catalog, the CIM Technology (CIMT) program "concentrates on the study of the individual subsystems such as materials handling systems, robotic systems, CNC machining, and automated metrology." [8] Courses in drafting fundamentals, materials and processes, software concepts, manufacturing networks, and computer simulation of manufacturing systems provide students with the opportunity to obtain either an associate or bachelor's degree and gain a foothold in the CIM job market.

Another form of specialized graduate education is available for United States military members through the services' graduate schools. The United States Air Force operates the Air Force Institute of Technology (AFIT) in Dayton, Ohio, at Wright-Patterson Air Force Base, and the U.S. Navy operates the Naval Postgraduate School at Monterey, California. Both schools offer computer engineering, information systems, and computer science programs similar to those at civilian universities, but the programs, projects, and course work tend to be oriented toward military applications. Nonetheless, this is an excellent way for military members to earn postgraduate degrees *at no expense* (other than incurring additional service time commitments to their respective services).

## Continuing Education and Adult Education–Oriented Programs

Chapter 9 discusses the concept of staying current with technological, business, and environmental changes. Pursuing continuing education through a variety of courses can be an important part of staying up to date. Most of this chapter deals with degree-oriented college and university education. However, continuing-education courses—those taken primarily to gain specific knowledge rather than pursue a degree—can round out further educational background without the often time-consuming, pressure-intensive environment of a degree program.

There are a number of means through which continuing education can be pursued. Various seminars and conferences (discussed in Chap. 9) can provide you with information about specific technologies and products. Most universities permit students to take individual graduate or undergraduate courses either for credit or on an auditing (no credit) basis. In addition, many colleges and universities have special adult education–oriented programs that offer courses in the evenings or on weekends. Evening courses are usually 3 or 4 hours per night, one night per week for a course, whereas some weekend programs tend to be all day Saturday and half a day the following Sunday. Many other schedule options are offered by the institutions that have adult education programs.

Another means by which continuing education can be pursued is through various satellite classroom programs. The National Technological University (NTU), headquartered in Fort Collins, Colorado, offers satellite hookup from many different universities to many different NTU "educational groundstations" around the United States. Through NTU courses, all of which are published in the NTU catalog, a student can attend, say, a database-modeling class from the University of Florida during regular working hours even though he or she may be physically located in Denver or Los Angeles or Pittsburgh. Graduate degrees are available from NTU as well.

## Succeeding in Graduate School

There are several different ways in which you can attend a graduate program in the computer field. Many professionals choose to attend school part-time or even full-time while retaining full-time employment, usually for financial reasons. Others, however, obtain masters' or doctoral degrees while attending school full-time, sometimes directly after completing undergraduate programs. For those in the latter category—and I am by no means suggesting that it is the preferred or better way, because either way is likely to be beneficial to your career—the following tips and recommendations will help you get the most from your graduate school experience.

It is possible, of course, to obtain a master's degree solely by completing the required curriculum and, if required by the department, writing a thesis or project paper. Doctoral degrees require classwork completion plus (usually) oral and written examinations and a dissertation, plus a certain amount of original research.

It is extremely desirable for anyone in a graduate program to be as involved as possible in his or her department's activities. That can include being a teaching assistant or a summer instructor, acting as a research assistant, attending in-house and external seminars and conferences, and coauthoring papers with faculty members. Just as we discussed in several of the preceding chapters, the more exposure you have to others in your organization and to people outside, the more your professional standing is enhanced.

In this particular circumstance (graduate school), teaching, research, and publication often relate directly to the number of job offers and accompanying salary offers, particularly if your chosen career is in academia or instruction. Demonstrated *high-quality* writing and teaching ability in a doctoral program is a direct indication of your abilities to be a tenure-rack assistant or associate professor.

Even in a master's program, these additional functions can be extremely valuable. First, and often foremost, you get paid for teaching and research; it's usually not a lot of money, but it can help. The benefits may be long- as well as short-term. When I was enrolled in the University of Arizona's M.S. program in management information systems, I designed an early systems requirement collection CASE tool and managed a 12-person implementation team. Six years later, after I had left the Air Force, that experience developing the prototype was a major factor in my being hired by Digital Equipment Corporation's database design CASE tool group. Similarly, I was also a teaching assistant in graduate school, and 8 years later I taught classes at the University of Denver; the graduate school experience was directly responsible for that opportunity.

As I mentioned, not everyone can—or wants to—earn a graduate degree in a full-time manner. For those who do, however, it is extremely beneficial to go beyond the minimum graduation requirements and benefit your career in the process.

## Doctoral Degrees: How Valuable Are They?

While we're on the subject of graduate school, let's take a minute to explore how valuable a doctoral degree is—or isn't—to your career path. The general rule, though some might argue with it, is that the more education and training you have the better, particularly if you're in a technical profession such as information systems. Many of the large, research-intensive organizations such as IBM, Digital Equipment, and AT&T put a premium on technical staff members with Ph.D. degrees in computer science or engineering. Several software engineering managers and product managers with whom I have worked over the years have earned doctoral degrees, yet they work in product development environments rather than research-intensive or academic areas.

Whether or not to pursue a doctoral degree is, and should be, a personal choice made in conjunction with your career planning. If your career plans include university teaching, large-scale software or hardware research, or other areas in which doctoral degrees are valued—if not required—you should have plans to pursue that degree at some opportune time in your career. Be advised, however, that many very successful people in the computer industry have been successful without doctoral degrees, so the pursuit and earning of that degree is not an automatic ticket to nor is it a prerequisite of success.

## Program Rankings

Everyone who has ever been associated with an academic environment, particularly a graduate program, is aware of the desire of university and college departments and programs to be able to say "we're number 1" in a particular area. Just as Harvard, Stanford, Wharton (University of Pennsylvania), and other top M.B.A. programs lay claim to various surveys that list them as number 1 or other high rank in their academic specialties, so computer science, artificial intelligence, and information systems programs point to similar surveys and rankings.

Keep in mind that different surveys base program rank on different criteria and use different selection and evaluation procedures. However, the available rankings, all culled from various trade publications, provide some guidelines for those considering undergraduate or graduate computer education. It is important to note that all the top programs cited below have their various strengths, and it would be advantageous, within any geographic constraints you might have, to try to match the *type* of program to your particular desires and goals. For example, in the information systems field, the University of Minnesota emphasizes skills needed to work in user organizations, and Georgia State University's program emphasizes a strong mix of practical applications and theoretical teaching.[9]

Let's look at a survey published in *Computerworld* in 1989 that listed the top 10 graduate programs in business-oriented information systems.[10] More than 250 corporate recruiters, academic professionals, and information systems executives were surveyed with respect to their IS programs. Two schools, Harvard and Stanford, were rated high on the strength of their M.B.A. programs but didn't have specific IS majors and were therefore excluded.

The top 10 programs and the reasons for their inclusion in the list were:

1. Massachusetts Institute of Technology (M.I.T.), on the strength of its research programs and its ability to place students in high-level positions

2. Georgia State University, with a strong mix of practical applications and theoretical teaching

3. University of Minnesota, with an emphasis on user organization skills

4. New York University, which has a youthful and diverse faculty that provides a wide variety of exposure for students

5. University of California at Los Angeles (UCLA), with a constantly evolving program designed to emphasize issues of current concern

6. University of Arizona (my alma mater), which has both an extremely technical IS program designed to give students career advantages and a high level of funded research

7. Indiana University, which emphasizes a real-life field project as a final course

8. University of Texas at Austin, with a balanced business and technical program that utilizes its Classroom 2000 facility

9. University of Pittsburgh, with a combined M.B.A. and M.S. program

10. University of Georgia, which features a multidisciplinary approach to IS in its management department to train students to work in user organizations as well as be computing specialists

## Representative Educational Programs

Chapter 3 touched briefly on typical educational backgrounds for each of the positions discussed. This section will explore, in more detail, various educational program alternatives for several of the job functions and career paths we've reviewed in previous chapters. By no means should the educational alternatives presented below be considered the best or the only ways to prepare for and succeed in a particular career orientation. For example, I knew a database tools product manager at a *Fortune* 100 computer manufacturer whose educational background was in quantum physics. Instead, the programs presented below are meant to be representative of typical educational backgrounds for the positions. For each of the three jobs, a set of job functions is listed in an attempt to match up each of the functions with various educational training items from the degree programs.

### Software development manager at a major hardware vendor

#### Job functions

1. Manage a group of 25 software development professionals, including 3 supervisors, who are developing an object-oriented database management system

2. Plan and execute staffing requirements for the entire program

3. Conduct performance appraisals; assign pay raises and promotions; and carry out any required disciplinary actions

4. Consolidate each group's development schedule into a single development plan

5. Coordinate development specifications and design documents with requirements provided by product marketing groups; negotiate any tradeoffs between features and time-to-market requirements

6. Prepare an annual capital budget for equipment and resource acquisition

### Education background

B.S., Computer Science

M.S., Computer Science

(Alt.) M.B.A. or M.S., Computer Information Systems

It would be most valuable for this manager to have undergraduate and graduate degrees from computer science programs that contained courses in operating systems, compilers, networks and communications, and basic hardware, along with a number of in-depth database classes. Since this manager's position is at a major hardware vendor, his or her career progression is likely to be directly affected by the depth of that person's technical background in a number of areas: not only the current emphasis on database management systems but also knowledge about the firm's operating systems, architectural environments, hardware platforms, and peripheral devices. This is usually true *whether or not* the current job (in this case, management) requires that knowledge.

Although some managers in this position may take a hands-off approach to the technical aspects of the project, it would be beneficial to be as familiar as possible with the many technical issues likely to arise. For example, many vendors today utilize a distributed development process whereby, say, a project such as this one might be developed by groups in more than one location. Very often, turf wars arise along geographical and other political boundaries and drag technical design and development issues into a mode of conflicting options. If this manager must be the decision maker between, for example, different options for doing SQL query optimization, it would be highly desirable to be as familiar as possible with the technical issues involved rather than have to rely on people whose motivations may be affected by other considerations. Therefore, the in-depth computer science background is likely to be critical to this manager's success in the current project as well as in future endeavors.

It is just as important, though, for someone with the listed responsibilities to be versed in a variety of management business subjects. An M.B.A. degree would be extremely valuable in addition to the M.S. in computer science, as would the business classes that usually go along with a CIS program. Even in the absence of a business-oriented degree, the manager should at a minimum have taken graduate-level courses in:

- *Personnel management.* Managing a group of 25 professionals requires great familiarity with personnel laws, including but not limited to equal opportunity laws, fair labor practices, and equal hiring practices. Reprimanding or dismissing employees also requires great sensitivity to the applicable regulations to ensure that the company is not liable in any legal action.

- *Organizational behavior and general management.* As we discussed in the preceding chapter, many organizations make the mistake of equating technical excellence with managerial ability and promote someone to responsibilities for which he or she is not fully prepared. A large number of behavioral dynamics are present in any group, particularly a large one, and a manager must be aware of them and know which are productive and which are not and be able to steer his or her organization toward the highest degree of productivity possible.

- *Corporate finance.* Capital budgeting and pay raise management require a basic understanding of corporate finance principles.

- *Marketing.* Any manager in charge of producing a product should understand such basic marketing principles as the importance of price, promotion, distribution, product features, and packaging for the times when feature tradeoffs must be made. Some high-cost features (in terms of development resources) may be more painful to include than some lower-cost ones, but the exclusion or deferment of the former may result in an unmarketable product. It might be argued that these decisions are better left to marketing people and product managers, but it helps immensely when the development manager can participate in the tradeoff process.

**Continuing education and training.**   This section is fairly standard for all of the careers we will look at in this section, as well as nearly every other computer career option (or, for that matter, nearly any other career path in *any* profession). It reads:

> Take as many classes and attend as many seminars and conferences as possible, not only in subjects directly applicable to your current job and anticipated next position, but in emerging areas of technology, general business, and in any subject of interest.

### Product manager at a spreadsheet software firm

#### Job functions

1. Gather and validate customer product requirements for current and future versions of the products

2. Manage internal and external (beta) product testing

3. Establish policies for all intellectual property protection, including patent, trademark, and copyright policies, in conjunction with the corporate attorneys

4. Manage export license requirements for foreign sales

5. Establish pricing and packaging strategies for the spreadsheet products

6. Negotiate all third-party relationships, including firms working on subcontracted development, add-on tools and utilities, and training and service organizations

7. Prepare volume, revenue, and earnings forecasts

8. Analyze competitive products in comparison with this firm's spreadsheet offerings

9. Establish hardware and operating system platform priorities for future versions of the firm's products

10. Coordinate all the above functions with the software development manager, marketing and sales directors, and senior corporate management

### Education background

B.S., Computer Information Systems

M.B.A.

(Alt.) B.S. or M.S., Computer Science

A product manager should have a broad background in technical matters—spreadsheet software in this instance—and in business and financial matters. A likely educational path for this product manager would be an undergraduate degree in CIS or a similar business-oriented computer curriculum with an M.B.A. degree. A product manager should be as technically astute as possible, but it isn't critical, for example, that a manager be able to determine the best way to design and implement spreadsheet macros or map screen output to a PostScript print driver, nor does he or she need to know the intricacies of implementing his or her spreadsheet product under a UNIX or Novell network environment. Instead, the successful product manager would look at the features of competitors' products and coordinate that information with market requirements and his or her firm's current product features. To accomplish those tasks, a basic understanding of the appropriate technologies is consolidated with his or her business training and experience in marketing, finance, accounting, and economics. A major part of a product manager's decision-making process consists of the ergonomics and user interfaces of the applicable products, so a strong educational background oriented toward the usability of software, such as a degree in CIS, would be extremely helpful.

**Continuing education and training.**   The same is true for a product manager as for a software development manager at a major hardware vendor.

### Tenure-track professor in a major university's MIS department

**Job functions**

1. Teach undergraduate and graduate MIS courses

2. Supervise research and dissertation projects of master's and doctoral students

3. Supervise teaching assistants

4. Represent the university, college, and department at major seminars, symposiums, and conferences

5. Publish articles and papers in areas of expertise

6. Apply for applicable public and private funding grants to support research

**Education background**

B.S., Computer Science

M.B.A. from a leading business school

Ph.D., Computer Information or Management Information Systems

Postgraduate study in computer-related or applications-oriented topics

Even though this individual will be teaching in a business-oriented computer department, it would be strongly beneficial to have as strong a technical—for example, computer *science*—background as possible. Students often request information in classroom or other settings which may be of a computer science nature more than in the CIS area. (For example: Why is the sorting algorithm in this PC database package so slow, and how could it be improved? This package uses a B*-tree index; would it be better using a hash table?) Any instructor, especially a university tenure-track assistant or associate professor, should have as much knowledge as possible to enhance his or her professional reputation. Remember that the lifeblood of a professor's career progression is student evaluations, and too many "I don't know" or "That's outside the scope of this subject" answers don't do much to enhance that instructor's credibility and resulting evaluations. More important than the direct result of evaluations is the effect on approval or disapproval of tenure (see Chap. 3).

An M.B.A. would be beneficial, since the professor's department is in the business college and there is often some degree of cross-communication with, for example, colleagues in the accounting department. He or she might teach an accounting course in computerized auditing environments or conduct an outside seminar with an accounting professor in the subject of evaluating personal computer accounting packages. In addition, the source of one's degree—the school at which it was earned—is usually very important in academia, so this professor's M.B.A. might best be earned from an Ivy League school, Stanford, Northwestern University, or other institution with a highly ranked M.B.A. program.

Finally, this professional's doctoral degree would probably best be earned in the area in which he or she will teach, namely, MIS or CIS. You might be wondering why this particular individual doesn't simply earn all of his or her bachelor's, master's, and doctoral degrees in CIS, since that subject contains elements of both computer science and business? The reason is that there is a high degree of overlap between undergraduate and graduate programs in this particular subject area. My bachelor's and master's degrees were in CIS and MIS, respectively, and I took nearly identical courses at both levels in database management systems, accounting, finance, marketing, and other subjects, and even used the same textbooks in some. Note, however, the *complementary* IS programs at King's College and the University of Arizona discussed earlier, which illustrate why looking carefully at the actual course work is important in choosing a program. As was mentioned before, someone in an academic environment should have as broad a background as possible, including different degrees at different levels, and have degrees from at least two different schools. Postdoctoral work is often a valuable addition as well, possibly in an area such as investment finance if the professor would like to concentrate his or her research in computer models for financial trading or a related subject.

**Continuing education and training.**   It is just as, if not more, important for an instructor to be as up to date as possible in subjects within his or her area as it is for any other computer professional. We briefly discussed postdoctoral work in the preceding section. Although some instructors do take formal courses, many rely on seminars and conferences as sources of information on current technical trends and accomplishments. In addition to attending conferences and seminars, presenting papers and being published in the proceedings is an excellent way to both stay current and enhance one's professional reputation, as well as earn outside consulting work.

## Summary

As noted in this chapter, there are a number of choices for undergraduate and graduate computer career education. Educational decisions, with respect to particular study tracks and institutions, should be made in conjunction with insight into your own interests and aptitudes, financial and geographic considerations, and perhaps most important, your career objectives. If taking 3 or 4 years to obtain a doctoral degree is financially feasible and critical to your career objectives, then that is a goal worth pursuing. If your goal is to develop computer systems for the health care industry, you should look into Stanford's medical information sciences program or a similar curriculum at another institution. Perhaps your goal is to be the manager of all product management and marketing activities at a large software vendor. In that case, an M.B.A. would be an extremely valuable asset in your career. Whatever your particular objectives are, education is an important part of the steps by which you can achieve them.

## Career Success Profile: Dr. Shamkant B. Navathe, Professor, College of Computing, Georgia Institute of Technology

### Education background

Ph.D, University of Michigan, Department of Industrial and Operations Engineering

New York University (NYU): Faculty of the Graduate School of Business Administration, 1975–1979

University of Florida: Faculty of the Computer Science Department, 1979–1990

Georgia Tech: Faculty of the College of Computing, 1990–present

### Professional affiliations

IBM World Trade, India, 1968–1969

Electronic Data Systems, 1971

IBM, summer work

Siemens, Germany, 1977

Visiting Research Faculty at Stanford University, Summer 1981

### Publications

Over 20 journal papers

Over 50 conference proceedings papers

Two textbooks, including databases and conceptual design

Editor or coeditor of five conference proceeding (ACM, IEEE, NYU) books

Sham Navathe is a leading academic expert on a number of information systems subjects, particularly those dealing with database management systems and data modeling. He has written over 70 journal and conference papers and two textbooks, and he has edited several other books. His background, unlike that of many academic professionals, includes extensive full-time and consulting work with major corporations, including IBM and Digital Equipment Corporation.

## Recommendations to others

**On pursuing an academic career.** "There are two increasingly divergent career tracks in academia. The predominant track is one that is research-oriented, through which one works at one of the 100–150 prestigious research universities and concentrates on conducting and sponsoring research programs. For this track, a Ph.D. (or equivalent doctoral degree) is a prerequisite and is necessary to pursue tenure.

"There is a complicating factor, though. Ph.D. production in computer science has increased threefold in the past couple of years; currently, 600 to 700 doctoral-level graduates enter the job market each year. The result of this increased production has been greatly increased competition for a dwindling number of academic openings, the latter caused primarily by stagnating university budgets.

"The consequence of these circumstances is the *requirement* for a newly graduated Ph.D. student to have a research and publication track record while still a student; without these items in a candidate's background, the chances of *obtaining* interviews are greatly diminished.

"A still further complicating factor is the quality of the publishing history. Doctoral students should try to publish in well-known, national or international conferences, rather than regional conferences. There is greater credibility and prestige for the former type of publishing than the latter, and this directly relates to employment opportunities.

"It is also beneficial for the Ph.D. graduate to have some demonstrated prototyping and development background and experience to complement theoretical knowledge. Universities are placing an increasing premium on the ability to teach real-life subjects, as well as theoretical ones.

"Summer employment with vendors or other organizations is another differentiator among the increasing number of candidates.

"When attending conferences, one should try to make as many contacts and meet as many people—particularly those in his or her area of specialization—as possible. This is a good way to gain name recognition, which is critical in academia.

"The alternate track is oriented toward teaching rather than research. Outside the realm of the research universities, there are hundreds of others whose primary task is to teach rather than conduct research. One can always move from a research track to a teaching one, but going in the opposite direction is extremely difficult if not impossible.

"For those who make the conscious decision to pursue a teaching-oriented career, teaching experience—such as being a graduate teaching assistant—is important.

"Many research-oriented schools have rotating appointments primarily for teaching (as opposed to research) to offset any shortages in experience and specialty areas among the research faculty. If, for example, a research university were to have only one or two faculty members with database experience but four or five courses in databases to be taught, then one or two teaching faculty members might work primarily with teaching those courses but not necessarily work on research. These types of appointments tend to be short-term—one or two years—and rarely result in tenure, but do represent a way to work at a prestigious university without having all of the prerequisite publication, research, and other background.

"There is also an annual Association for Computing Machinery (ACM) Computer Science Conference (CSC), usually held in the February–March timeframe, that functions as an employment exchange for the teaching-oriented colleges and universities. Those considering a teaching career would be well-advised to attend this conference.

"Once employed in a research capacity, faculty members should strive to publish in several major publications each and every year. The hard facts are that 30 to 50 percent of those who spend six years in an academic capacity *don't* get accepted for tenure, and thus usually move on to another school to begin the tenure pursuit again."

**On computer education.** "Schools have different programs in computer science and the other information disciplines. At the University of Florida, for example, there are three different tracks, all under the administration of the engineering department. By contrast, Georgia Tech has an independent College of Computing, with its own set of academic tracks. You will probably continue to see more mixtures of courses and degree tracks.

"Different types of programs also have different accreditation procedures. Computer engineering, being an offshoot of electrical engineering, has different accreditation policies than MIS does. Prospective students should always check and ensure that the particular program of interest has the appropriate accreditations."

# End Notes

1. *King's College 1990–1991 Catalog*, pp. 40–42.
2. *The University of Arizona Record Graduate Catalog, 1989–1990 and 1990–1991*, p. 104.
3. Ibid, p. 104.
4. *Stanford University Bulletin Courses and Degrees, 1990–1991*, pp. 136–137.
5. *Penn State 1990–1991 Baccalaureate Degree Programs Bulletin*, pp. 358–359.
6. Ibid, pp. 357–358.
7. *Stanford University Bulletin Courses and Degrees, 1990–1991*, pp. 697–701.
8. *Purdue University Bulletin: School of Technology Catalog*, pp. 44–45.
9. "MIT, Georgia State lead IS honor roll," *Computerworld*, Oct. 30, 1989, p. 1.
10. Ibid, p. 1.

# 7

# Additional
# Career Options

Chapter 5 discussed the many options you, as a computer professional, have with respect to your career path. This chapter focuses on additional career options, mostly out of the mainstream of full-time, "in the office" career alternatives. As your lifestyle, professional goals, and monetary needs change over time, you might consider one or more of these options to be woven into your overall career plan.

## Part-Time Work and Job Sharing

There often comes a time in their lives when people find themselves torn between the pursuit of a career and the lure of other activities and interests. Much has been made in recent years about "mommy track" career paths, which allow women in the business, technical, and professional realms who might not wish to be on the fast track to the executive suite to balance their professional and family lives. A corollary "daddy track" exists, with much resistance from many career-oriented senior managers, for men who also wish to provide some balance in their lives. Debate still rages as to the merits and problems of these types of career paths, but one fact is certain and directly applies to career choices: For many different reasons, both men and women in the computer industry (as well as every other type of profession) often choose to throttle back the velocity at which their careers are progressing.

One choice that permits and supports such an approach to career planning is to work part time. Many jobs in the computer industry that we discussed in Chap. 3 are difficult to adapt to part-time work, such as being a senior vice president of information systems or a director of product management; but most of the positions are readily adapted to it. Teaching, developing software, technical writing, consulting, and other jobs provide the opportunity for someone to work a variable number of hours and a flexible schedule in accordance with family and other needs. Part-time work may be done on your own on a contract or consulting basis, or it may be done in the employ of a computer vendor, *Fortune* 500 corporation, or a mid-size company. A wide variety of options are available to part-timers.

A variation of part-time work is *job sharing*. Many large organizations permit two or more people to actually share a particular position on preagreed terms. For example, two software developers who share a single development position might each work 4 hours per day or trade full 8-hour days on and off with each other. A set of development tasks and responsibilities is assigned to that position, and the two developers work together as if they were one individual to design, code, test, and implement their software. The same concept may be applicable to technical writers, customer support specialists, and many of the positions that are adaptable to part-time work.

What are the ramifications of part-time work or job sharing on your career? One of the complaints about mommy-track careers is that, although the concept itself provides more options to professionals than (1) you work full-time or (2) you don't work, there often is a stigma attached to someone who opts for this career path. Others may question the commitment of that individual to the good of the organization. As many people who have pursued it have shown, though, the time away from a job and an organization often provides just the right amount of refreshment and a new outlook, permitting them to be extremely productive upon their return to full-time work.

It is best to assess your own organization's climate and culture (see Chap. 4) with respect to willingness to support a mommy- or daddy-track career. If, for example, the senior vice president of marketing took 2 years off from full-time work when she had twins, there might be a greater possibility that your own desire to take time off will not hurt your career prospects than if your entire senior management is made up of former military officers who collectively endured many years away from their families while on remote assignments. As with many other topics discussed in this book, assess your environment and situation as carefully as possible to determine the best course of action to take.

## Returning to School

Many computer professionals attend graduate school directly after completing their undergraduate degrees; others pursue continuing education on a part-time basis while being employed full-time; and still others elect to pursue further full-time education—undergraduate or graduate—at some point down their career path. This decision and its effects on careers are very similar to those of part-time work discussed in the preceding section. Earning a doctoral degree, for example, might be a beneficial move if you would eventually like to pursue a career in university education, but it may or may not help your career path in industry. That does not mean, however, that anyone who covets a senior management position at some point in the future should avoid career sidetracks into the educational realm. Many people enjoy the learning process and can use educational time in much the same manner as any other time away from a high-pressure corporate environment: to attain new perspectives and renewed vigor toward their jobs and careers. If 2 or 3 years spent pursuing additional education is financially feasible, there is no reason it shouldn't be considered in your career planning.

## Telecommuting

The computer industry is tailor-made for telecommuting, or working primarily from your home. There are some positions in which it is difficult to succeed while telecommuting, particularly those that require a great deal of face-to-face contact with others in your organization. For technical writers, software developers, and similar professionals, though, working at home can be far more productive than facing long, draining commutes through massive traffic jams on a daily basis. Telecommuting is most popular in such areas as Los Angeles, San Francisco, New York City, Boston, and similar metropolitan areas where people often spend 4 or 5 hours *per day* in traffic. Telecommuting provides a mechanism by which most job functions can be performed at home, with office appearances required only at periodic intervals.

A number of resources are required for telecommuters to be as productive as possible. At a minimum, each person should have a terminal, modem, and separate telephone line through which communications to an office-based computer system can be achieved, as well as word processing, spreadsheet, and other software required to perform the job functions. Electronic mail and other office productivity software provide additional means of communication between telecommuters and their colleagues who are office-based. Optimally, software developers should have some form of high-powered personal computer or workstation, particularly if the software they are developing requires graphics user interfaces (GUIs). In order to be able to test their software productively, they need access to the same resources, or at least down-scaled versions, as their target environments. With the growth of client-server computing and other forms of distributed processing, home-bound workstations can often take advantage of the resources of corporate mainframes and other computing facilities in a relatively easy manner.

## Invent a Job

If you don't find a position described in Chap. 3 or some other position peripherally related to the computer field to your liking, invent a job. The 1980s supposedly was the birth of a service-based economy in which services (as opposed to goods) became ever-increasingly important to the economies of the world. The early years of that decade saw the explosive growth not only of personal computers and other technologies but also magazines, newsletters, on-line services, and other resources dedicated to the explanation and support of the new technologies. Many of the newsletters and periodicals started during that time have since folded or been incorporated into other publications, but others prospered and provided their founders with a great deal of professional and financial reward.

If, for example, you are an expert in neural network technology but are tired of software development in a full-time corporate or university environment, you might consider starting a monthly or quarterly newsletter devoted to, say, applied neural networks for business environments. Will it succeed? It depends on the need in the marketplace for such a newsletter as well as your own marketing and technical successes in its publication. There is no reason, however, not to pursue such an endeavor if you believe it will be successful, your research indicates that it will be, *and it's what you want to do.* If it succeeds, that will be wonderful. If it does not, you can at least say that you tried and then look at your next career option.

## Sabbaticals

We discussed time off from the computer industry briefly in Chap. 2 with respect to voluntary or involuntary termination and what options then existed. There is no reason why you can't take time off from your profession even if your job security isn't being threatened. Some organizations actively support, encourage, and pay salaries during sabbaticals of varying lengths; others permit unpaid time away from the corporate environment.

There are many ways in which you can use a sabbatical: volunteer work, travel, politics, or just rejuvenating yourself, to name a few. If you have been an office-bound worker your entire life, you might find

3 months of outside, physical labor building an addition to your house to be an invigorating experience. Volunteering to help disabled patients in a hospital or children in a school for the disadvantaged learn to use a personal computer may give you an entire new outlook on the relative importance of your life's work. That is not meant to sound "preachy"; it comes from personal experience. Time spent helping others lets you put staff meetings and other burdens and pressures of organizational climates into perspective and helps you bear with previously intolerable facets of your professional life.

## Summary

Your career path is more than just a projected series of jobs and positions in various types of organizations. It encompasses other facets of your life which may, at various junctions, encourage you to pursue an untraditional form of employment or involvement in the computer industry. Just as you have a wide variety of positions, organizational environments, educational alternatives, and technologies from which to choose and combine with each other, so you have a number of career alternatives that may best fit your lifestyle and needs at some points in your life. The key is to expand your horizons and not be tied down by preconceived notions or others' expectations of what *you* should be doing at those points in your career. At times, you may wish to pursue part-time work, take time off from the field altogether, or chase some other goal or dream.

## Career Success Profile: Dr. Alan Rose, President, Multiscience Press, Inc.

### Education background

B.A., University of Pennsylvania, 1960

Ph.D, Indiana University, 1970

### Career

Professor of English, University of New Hampshire, 1969–1976

Editor, Davis Publications, 1976–1981

President, Multiscience Press, 1981–present

Alan Rose is president of Multiscience Press, Inc., a publishing firm which copublishes professional computer science and engineering books. Multiscience Press acts as a "total concept" book publisher and also functions as a packager of camera-ready pages for trade computer paperbacks.

Following his time in an academic environment, Dr. Rose entered the publishing field, first working with Davis Publications before founding his own publishing firm in 1981, which coincided with the boom in both personal computers and books about the many hardware and software subjects. Dr. Rose's firm works with a number of major New York publishers, including McGraw-Hill. His publishing firm is a perfect example of what is emphasized in this chapter—and in this book in general—with respect to seizing the initiative in one's career in the computer field, even if it means pursuing an unconventional path such as founding one's own computer book publishing house.

### Best career move

"Founding my own company."

### Recommendations for others

**On conceiving and writing books.**   "One should be aware of the extent and difficulty of the undertaking; allow enough time for any book development project. Such projects should be integrated into one's current career, and complement other work being done at that time.

"Writers should also be *very* firm with themselves about completing projects. These book projects should not be treated lightly nor secondarily to one's primary job functions; manuscript submission dates and other deadlines should be viewed in the same light as those in software development or whatever one's primary tasks are."

**On careers in the publishing field.**   "There is a very limited number of jobs in computer book editing, as well as a relatively small turnover of the people in those positions. Also, one should be prepared for the implications of the phenomenon that practically everybody in the publishing business knows everyone else; there are few secrets in the computer book publishing industry. Factors such as these should be carefully considered if one wishes to pursue a career in publishing."

**General.**   "Be realistic and flexible about the possibility of changing careers. It can be done successfully, and often can turn out to be an excellent boost to one's professional life, but contingency plans should always be considered."

# 8

# Hot Areas
# for the 1990s

The preceding chapters have emphasized that your career success, particularly in less than robust economic times, can often be increased by concentrating your efforts in areas of technology and applications that show the most promising chances for growth. As was mentioned in Chap. 1, any list of the most promising areas of technologies and applications will change often, and it is best to survey and study these subjects at regular intervals to ensure that your career is oriented toward the areas that are the most promising at any point.

The technology areas listed below are not in any special order, but they represent the top 10 areas likely to be promising platforms for your career. This list was consolidated from personal experience and observation, as well as from numerous industry and trade periodicals.

## Technology Areas

### Security

Long a concern of financial and government organizations, the computer security field exploded in the late 1980s with the advent of widespread computer virus outbreaks and other security infringements. Many large and midsize organizations—business, government, and education—have or plan to utilize computer security consultants and in-house staff to ensure that their operations are not disrupted or permanently disabled by external and internal assaults on their computing resources. Computer security specializations are expected to continue to grow into the next decade.

There are many aspects of a computer career oriented toward computer security, from developing specialized encrypting and decrypting hardware devices to writing security-sensitive software and from specializing in computer center disaster preparedness and recovery to building a consulting practice around auditing organizations' computer security practices. Nearly every one of the job functions and career paths discussed in the preceding chapters can be oriented toward an emphasis on security.

### Networks and communications

The 1980s also brought about a boom in computer communications. The continuing personal computer revolution led many organizations to incorporate local area networks to allow their computers to communicate among themselves and share such resources as printers and file servers. Long-haul communication also continued to grow as traditional barriers were overcome through enhanced value-added wide area networks. The next decade promises similar growth in various network and communications architectures and products, particularly in the area of systems integration (see the next section).

There are many parts of the network and communication area in which you can concentrate your efforts:

- *Developing protocol drivers and interfaces.* Any device or software component which is to communicate over a communication network must have its own protocol drivers or utilize those available through preexisting resources. Expertise in layered protocols and the required interfaces at each layer is a valuable asset to have in your skill set.

- *Network design.* Designing local area and wide area networks can be a complex task when many different nodes, gateways, bridges, routers, and topology alternatives are applicable. Minimized traffic routing, alternative communication paths, and other design considerations can mean a significant amount of savings—or unnecessary expenditures—depending on the quality of the network design.

- *Network migration.* As organizations' hardware environments evolve, new network and communication solutions are often needed. Migrating an organization's network and communication facilities, including physical media, network interface devices, terminal drivers, and other components of the communications environment can be a very difficult task, particularly if real-time operations cannot be disrupted during the migration process. Specialists in this area must ensure that the operations of a business or other organization are not hindered by the necessary technical evolution.

### Systems integration

As organizations continue to integrate heterogeneous hardware, operating systems, and applications software into the same computing environments, the desire to share information among these diverse platforms has led to the multibillion dollar field of computer systems integration. For example, a client may wish to incorporate spreadsheet figures, graphics software charts, and database information into a word processing document, transfer the compound document to a file server that utilizes a different operating system, and electronically mail it to a selected distribution list. Although applications are now available to meet such requirements, many customers wish to utilize their existing investments in various software packages which may be incompatible to various degrees with one another. Systems integration professionals assist organizations in achieving an integrated computing environment across diverse platforms by performing such services as finding and installing special integration software or sometimes writing transparent interface drivers. The consolidation of the computer industry to several operating system platforms such as MS-DOS, OS/2, UNIX, VMS, and MVS will greatly increase the desire of organizations to share information among applications and various hardware utilizing these quasi-standard operating systems, and the need for consulting and in-house expertise in this area will dramatically increase. Many large companies, including AT&T, Digital Equipment Corporation, and UNISYS, offer systems integration services that assist users in integrating "foreign" systems into their environments. Other firms, such as General Motors Electronic Data Systems (EDS) and Perot Data Systems, are major "nonpartisan" participants in the systems integration business. There is, however, plenty of room for individuals or small consulting firms, particularly in niche markets.

### Database systems

Surprisingly, many large organizations still base their information systems on "flat files" or older database technology such as hierarchical or network model systems. As relational technology continues to mature and improve in performance, more and more companies are implementing new applications and migrating existing ones to relational database management systems. There are several areas of database technology that will be heavily utilized into the next decade, including, but not limited to:

- *Data modeling.* Using entity relationship or other conceptual modeling techniques to analyze users' database requirements and create a non-implementation-specific model of their database.

- *Database tuning.* Helping users reorganize existing database implementations to take better advantage of data access patterns and improve user retrieval and storage response.

- *Distributed databases.* Both homogeneous (same DBMS across nodes) and heterogeneous (different DBMSs) distributed database technology will mature and become widespread during the 1990s. Very few computer professionals have much experience with distributed databases aside from classroom theory; those who become recognized experts in this technology will have a large potential clientele among large and medium-size organizations.

- *Object-oriented databases.* Many applications and environments are better suited to object-oriented databases (OODBs) than relational implementations. There isn't a great deal of expertise in OODBs available due to their relative newness in the database solution space, and specialists in OODBs as well as other object-oriented programming and development techniques are likely to be in great demand in the years ahead.

## CASE tools

"Software engineering" became one of the great buzzwords of the 1980s as an outgrowth of structured programming (one of the great buzzwords of the 1970s) with government and business firms trying to get a handle on developing and maintaining large and complex computer systems. Along with software engineering practices, many organizations began experimenting with computer-aided software engineering (CASE) tools, which attempt to assist users with (depending on the tool set) many aspects of the systems life cycle: requirements collection, systems specification, systems design, applications development, systems operation, and systems maintenance. Graphics CASE tools, especially workstation-based ones, assist users with such tasks as drawing data flow and entity-relationship diagrams, creating program structure charts, and generating computer code data definitions (and sometimes procedural code). The commercial CASE tools market is relatively new, despite the fact that university-based research and prototype development has been going on for over a decade. As the CASE tool market expands, organizations will want to get the most out of their investment in that technology. A career specializing in integrating CASE tools into an organization's development methodologies will continue to be in demand in the 1990s.

A "subspecialty" of CASE technology is integrating various CASE tools, including those from different vendors, into a single life cycle management system. Various prototypes of these life cycle management systems have been available for several years, but they have lacked much of the power and performance required, particularly in repository and dictionary management. Major efforts are underway at a number of CASE tools vendors to provide repository-based CASE tools integration platforms, and, as with CASE tools in general, a career oriented toward this specialty is likely to be successful.

### Expert systems

One of the most promising commercial aspects of artificial intelligence is the use of expert systems shells such as Nexpert Object and KEE to develop intelligent, rule-based applications. An expert system shell functions in much the same way as a database management system in that it provides a predefined set of services to which the user can fit his or her data and operations, the result being one or more computer applications. The primary distinction between a rule-based application and a traditional one, however, is that the logic of the former is encoded in the data and information, often in the form of "operations upon objects" (to borrow from object-oriented terminology) rather than encoded in procedural programs as in the latter. Expert systems technology is still relatively new, and such recent advances as extending the rule base to interface with relational databases promise to provide an alternative development platform base for selected applications. Expert systems specialists—those who understand both expert systems technology and general applications development principles—can serve as "knowledge engineers" and assist users with choosing an applicable expert system shell (e.g., does the shell support forward chaining? backward chaining? both?) and developing the rule base for the shell.

### UNIX

The last years of the 1980s brought about tremendous interest in the UNIX area, primarily fueled by the quest for "open systems." As most organizations, even those traditionally bound to IBM mainframe environments, attempt to integrate UNIX into their computing environments, knowledge about and experience with UNIX is a valuable addition to anyone's skill set. At a minimum, understanding the difference between the variants of UNIX—System V, OSF, BSD, and their mutations such as Open Look and SCO—is an important way to position your career toward your own organization's technological forefronts.

## Multimedia computing

Few commercial applications today can be truly considered to be multimedia systems, that is, systems taking full advantage of not only screen and print data but also voice, sound, and motion. This will likely change in the current decade, since the price of multimedia hardware is constantly being lowered, and various platforms and tools will make it much easier than it is today to develop multimedia applications and systems. A thorough understanding of multimedia hardware and software, as well as insight into how multimedia applications can best be designed to take advantage of that technology, is another promising emphasis for your career success.

## Disaster planning and management

Discussed briefly under Security, disaster planning and management has grown to be a specialization by itself. Many of the factors crucially important to data center and operations security—natural disasters, terrorist actions, and internal sabotage—must be considered and counterplans must be developed to ensure that critical company operations are not interrupted and company revenues and assets not dramatically and adversely affected. This is an extremely promising area for a consulting specialty, because smaller organizations are more likely to utilize outside consulting advice in this area than to hire in-house specialists.

## Systems migration

Migrating applications and systems is one of the most difficult tasks (along with systems integration) that a computer professional can undertake.[1] Systems migration combines the most difficult aspects of new systems development and applications maintenance into a singular, highly constrained, and high-pressure environment. For example, the advent of such technology as client-server systems has many mainframe-oriented organizations scrambling to convert mainframe-based, third-generation–language (e.g., COBOL) applications to distributed, client-server applications built around fourth-generation languages (4GLs) for improved performance and easier maintainability than their current environments. Consultants and in-house specialists must be intimately familiar with both the source and target environments (both hardware and operating system), code conversion techniques, multiple job control languages and runstream management systems, system calls, and a myriad of other items. Careers built around systems and applications migration will continue to be promising in the 1990s as well as today.

## Applications Areas

A complete list of all applications areas of emphasis for the 1990s would be too exhaustive for this book but you may find the following useful for your career orientation.

### Medical and health care systems

Much has been written about the health care cost crisis around the world, particularly in the United States. One of the outcomes of this situation has been the advent of a variety of medical and health care information systems covering many areas from hospital and medical practice management (accounting, billing, and scheduling) to a variety of clinical systems, including patient care, laboratory, radiology, and pharmacy. It is expected that this applications area will continue to grow rapidly in terms of interest and the need for new systems development and management. Any of the technology areas listed previously in this chapter can be oriented toward medical and health care systems.

### Civilian government systems

The 1980s saw explosive growth in defense and military computer systems, which were an integral part of the United States military buildup. The 1990s are expected to see similar growth in civilian government systems not only at the United States federal level but at state and local levels as well. The same will be true in many countries around the world as well.

In the United States, for example, the Internal Revenue Service is embarking on a major multistate and multiyear effort to develop a new tax and revenue management system. Despite job cutbacks at most federal government agencies, the IRS plans to expand its in-house staff and supplement its staff with contractor and consultant help. The Federal Aviation Administration is attempting to enhance both air traffic and ground traffic radar-based computer systems at most major United States airports. The Social Security Administration also has major automation efforts under way. The Pennsylvania Department of Welfare plans to update its major computing system, as do many other departments in that and other states.

What does this trend mean to your computer career? If you are inclined toward employment in a government organization or a contractor specializing in government clients, you might be well advised to consider emphasizing civilian agencies or their contractors, at least in the upcoming years. Although opportunities will certainly be available in the defense industry and defense-oriented government agencies in the United States in the 1990s, the growth in those areas is not likely to be as rapid or as smooth as in civilian government sectors.

## Summary

The lists of technology and applications areas presented are not meant to be a definitive statement of "this is how you should orient your career right now." Rather, they are meant as guidelines to help you determine specific areas of technology, and the applications to which they might be applied, that might be applicable to your background and interests.

As was mentioned in Chap. 1, these items should be factored together with organizational environments, specific job duties, education and training, and your desired career path, the outcome hopefully being your successful career.

## Career Success Profile: Jeffrey Winwood, Branch Manager, Robert Half/Accountemps of Denver

### Education background

Pace University, New York

### Career

Executive search firm specializing in information systems recruiting, New York, 1982–1983

Executive search firm specializing in information systems recruiting for banking and brokerage industries, New York, 1983–1984

Operated own executive search firm on Wall Street and also specialized in information systems for banking and brokerage industries, 1984–1989

Branch Manager, Robert Half/Accountemps of Denver, 1989–present

Jeffrey Winwood manages all Robert Half operations in the Denver office. He has been in the executive recruiting industry for 10 years, most of which was spent on Wall Street in the quick-pulsed days of the 1980s. He is a good example of maintaining flexibility in one's career path and factoring in the external economic climate into one's career decision making, having both started his own firm and moved to one of the largest international recruiting firms in the information systems career area, two moves that were timed extremely well.

## Long-term career objectives

To grow with Robert Half International in executive recruiting management.

## Best career move

Starting and operating his own business. "I learned a lot in those five years on Wall Street, particularly working in an 'old network' environment." He built a sound reputation in the executive recruiting industry, paving his way to his current position at Robert Half.

## What he would change

Completing his degree at Pace University when he was younger.

## Recommendations for others

**General.** "Stay technically astute, on the leading edge of hardware, software, and communications technology. This is true even after promotions into management; the managers being cut in slowdowns are those most behind the times with respect to the state of the art in computer technology. Companies that have a choice between keeping a technically competent manager and one without that technical background usually opt to keep the former.

"Professionals should try to be diversified in the types of applications and user industries in which they can work. Banking and brokerage industries were very active several years ago while I was in New York, but the slowdowns there have meant that those able to move into, for example, a manufacturing environment have been able to stay on their career paths while those unable to adapt have been sidetracked. It is also important, though, not to jump around too much, spending a year or so in insurance, then defense, then accounting, and so on. Moves should be planned very carefully."

**On making a career move.** "The most prevalent reason to consider a career move is lack of growth opportunities, both in the technology someone is using and within their present organization itself. If the current climate of technology at the company dictates that someone will be a COBOL programmer on a System/36 for the next five years, with no moves towards AS/400s and other newer technologies, *and* there are no promotion opportunities into management, it is probably time to consider a change.

"Salary and compensation are secondary to growth opportunities. The true career person knows that the money will be there: if not immediately, then eventually. Making moves on a purely monetary basis will often catch up with people, and lead them into career traps and dead-ends."

**On the executive recruiting industry.**     "Executive recruiters have to enjoy working with people. They have to be good listeners first, since they are really matchmakers between client companies and those searching for employment opportunities. They also have to have good communications skills, being able to convey to a client *why* a person will be that perfect match for an open position.

"They must also be assertive and aggressive. People in this industry sink or swim on their own. There is a lot of marketing, and recruiting of both client companies and professionals. A lot of the most highly qualified people don't answer classified advertisements; recruiters try to know who is who in this industry, especially in their current geography, and seek them out when applicable.

"Honesty and integrity are also very important. Both good and bad reputations stick, since it is a small world. Investment in people is also important. Some recruiters won't spend time with an entry-level, trainee person since they can't make much, if any, money off placing that person. However, a good recruiter will take that time now, knowing that four or five years down the road that person will likely be more highly qualified, and will remember the people who took the time at the beginning with them. [Author's note: The same is true of computer consultants, and anyone else who must build a business base. Remember this!]

"Insight is important. If a company wants a designer with coding experience, don't send them applicants who haven't coded in ten years. Résumés must be reviewed carefully, and the exact abilities of applicants drawn out, since most résumés tend to be somewhat poorly written.

"If a recruiter has no computer background, he or she can learn a lot about the industry from reading résumés, looking at the matches between technologies, as well as from reading advertisements. Even if you never have been, for example, an MVS COBOL developer, you can learn from résumés and advertisements that JCL skills are crucial for a successful IBM mainframe developer. You don't have to be perceived by your client companies as a 'know it all'; instead, they will respect your asking the appropriate questions to help determine exactly the type of candidate who will fit their needs. Ask questions about the exact nature of their corporate climate and other not-so-obvious things.

"The recruiting field has the potential to highly compensate those that are successful, but there is also a lot of burnout from high-stress situations. Therefore, there is always room for people coming into this field from other areas of computing and from other job fields."

## End Note

1. Alan R. Simon and Ted Davis, *Applications Migration: IBM to VAX,* Van Nostrand Reinhold, New York, 1991.

# 9

# Supplemental Information

In this final chapter, we'll look at a variety of supplemental topics with respect to your career in the computer profession. Many of this chapter's topics, particularly those related to the job-searching process, offer a number of sources of further information, including articles and entire books. It is highly advisable, after reviewing this chapter's content, to pursue applicable information in the references provided.

## Staying Current[1]

Everyone in the computer field has probably experienced the frustration of finally thinking that he or she has a handle on a particular area of technology—say, PC-based database management systems—only to pick up a copy of a computer trade magazine and see a headline such as "Five New Client-Server DBMS Products for OS/2." Truly, the learning process never ends.

The obvious fact is that the computer industry is so dynamic that a concerted effort is required to keep abreast of new technologies and products. That is especially true for computer consultants, who can't afford not to be aware of the latest products and offerings in their areas of specialization.

Here we will discuss how to keep your knowledge as current as possible in the areas of computer technology, business, and career-related topics. We will look at some of the many periodicals available and discuss their appropriateness to your career. We'll also look at the many other sources of information available to you.

## Periodicals

It is literally impossible to read every periodical in the computer, business, and career areas. Without a doubt, 50 hours per week or more

**TABLE 9.1    Representative No-Cost Periodicals**

| | |
|---|---|
| *Datamation* | *SunExpert* |
| *Software Magazine* | *SunTech Journal* |
| *Digital Review* | *UNIX Review* |
| *DEC Professional* | *Network World* |
| *PC Week* | *Systems Integration* |

could be devoted to nothing but reading and research. A technique that I use is to subscribe to many different magazines and newspapers (many of them *free,* as you will soon see), scan them upon receipt, note the most important and applicable articles and stories, and file them in either of my offices. I usually can recall that, for example, I skimmed an article about a particular CASE tool sometime within the past 6 months, and I can then search through my files to locate that article when necessary. Other stories of interest I will read at length, especially if they are critical to work I am doing at that particular time.

Many periodicals can be obtained absolutely free, the only cost being 10 minutes or so every year to fill out another qualifying subscription card (Table 9.1). Other periodicals, such as *Computerworld* and *BYTE,* do charge for a subscription, but they contain much valuable information. There are specialized magazines for nearly every type of computer system from PCs to supercomputers, and nearly every area of technology such as data communications and artificial intelligence.

Business information can be obtained from "the big four," *The Wall Street Journal, Forbes, Fortune,* and *Business Week,* as well as a host of other business and financial periodicals. I find a lot of good information about the computer industry and business in general in *Financial World,* as well as small business information in *Inc.* magazine.

There are also a number of highly specialized newsletters, usually carrying high subscription prices ($200 or more) in areas of CASE and database. If you specialize in one of those areas, you might investigate a trial subscription to see if you can obtain additional information of value to you.

Career information can be obtained from a number of sources. *Computerworld* has a weekly column on career-related topics, as well as frequent charts and graphs about salary compensation, hiring trends in various industries, and other subjects. The business periodicals mentioned earlier often feature stories about employment trends by industry and geography. *The National Employment Business Weekly* (NEBW) has a number of articles about interviewing, résumé writing, job searching, and other career-related topics, as well as many different display advertisements for positions. In addition, collections of NEBW articles can be found in *The Best of the National Employment Business Weekly,* a series of 12 booklets. These booklets include collections of articles about on-the-job strategies, résumé and letter writing, perspectives on relocation, and barriers to employment, among other topics, and are available mailorder from NEBW.

## Books

There are a number of books available in every area of computer technology. When you find you need more information than you can consolidate from periodicals about CASE, SQL, Novell NetWare, UNIX, or any other subject, you can always find one or more books about your subject. The same is true of business subjects. If you need to learn more about finance, marketing, accounting, or small business operations, there are a number of sources.

Similarly, a large number of books discuss career-related topics. Some, such as *What Color Is Your Parachute?*, by Richard Nelson Bolles, help you explore exactly where you can go with respect to your career and your life as a whole, and it can be very helpful in gaining the critical insight that I have stressed throughout this book.

## Education

Chapter 6 discussed computer education in great detail, including the concept of continuing education. As you progress in your career, time more and more becomes a valuable commodity, and it seems there is never enough time for pursuit of further education. I would strongly recommend that you make the time, particularly if you find yourself working with rapidly obsolescent technology or stuck in a stagnant career position. The incremental technical or business education may be the career lifesaver that you need.

## Seminars and conferences

An alternative to formal, classroom-based education is attending seminars on technical, professional, and business topics. A number of organizations, such as Digital Consulting and Learning Tree, offer a wide variety of seminars about up-and-coming technologies and products that can provide you with valuable information in a short time. Conferences sponsored by organizations such as the Association for Computing Machinery (ACM) provide you with similar opportunities to further your knowledge.

## User's groups

Groups of people who have hardware and software in common are an excellent way to meet with others who use technology similar to that you use. There are user's groups for microcomputers and PC software packages, as well as large MIS-oriented groups such as the DEC User's Symposium (DECUS).

### Professional organizations

Many cities have active chapters of the Association for Computing Machinery (ACM), Data Processing Management Association (DPMA), or similar professional organizations. You may want to join one of these groups, both for the information you can obtain in the technical arena and the professional and career-oriented contacts.

### Vendor mailing lists

Sometimes the vast amount of unsolicited product information you receive from vendors can seem like a major pain. However, an occasional gem will turn up and help you solve a particularly tricky technical problem or otherwise help you in your current job.

## Résumé Basics

The first thing to realize about résumés is that there are countless "expert" opinions as to what constitutes a "good" résumé as opposed to a "bad" one.

"It must be two pages or less in length," shouts one camp.

"Nonsense; it should be as long or as short as necessary to market your abilities," retorts the other side.

"Educational background should go first."

"Nope; it should be your career summary."

"You should *always* have a stated objective at the beginning."

"Leave off the 'objective' portion; make it general enough so it doesn't freeze you out of a job for which you would be suited."

"Include a salary history, references, and outside activities."

"Don't include a salary history, references, or outside activities."

And it goes on and on. My own personal opinion—and I stress that it is only my opinion—is that you should develop a résumé that fits your own strengths and downplays any shortcomings. There are certainly rules and guidelines that help you market your skills, but there are really no hard-and-fast rules for the format, number of pages, and overall content. Countless sources are available to provide you with guidance in preparing your résumé and many samples from which you can tailor your own. The following are my simple rules, which have proved effective in my various searches over the years:

1. *Include real accomplishments.* Don't just list your job title and superficial job description duties. Describe what you accomplished: the systems you developed, the contracts you won, the money you

saved, and other items which illustrate that you haven't just been marking time in your preceding positions.

2. *Include real monetary figures when possible.* Businesses exist to earn a profit. If you have influenced, directly or indirectly, earnings or cost reductions, say so.

3. *Show diversity when possible.* Demonstrate that you have a background and experience in both technology and business. Show that you know a number of different computer languages, operating systems, and most important, state-of-the-art technologies.

4. *Ensure that the printed result is aesthetically pleasing.* Although content is your résumé's most important aspect, the importance of appearance cannot be overstated. The easy access to laser printers provides everyone with the means to tailor an attractive, professional-looking résumé. Although an attractive résumé won't land you an interview by itself, an unattractive one may just keep you from getting that interview in the first place.

5. *Don't lie or exaggerate.* Lies and exaggerations *will* catch up with you. Emphasize, but don't invent, your accomplishments.

Figure 9.1 illustrates a sample résumé. As I mentioned before, this is not intended to be a definitive statement as to the content of a résumé. The sample does illustrate the points made above with respect to highlighting accomplishments, including monetary figures, and showing a diversity of skills and other aspects of one's background.

## Job Search Basics

Since entire books are written on the process of searching for employment, I will only attempt to summarize, in a concise manner, some of the key components of the job search.

### Where to find information

One of the worst mistakes anyone can make is to assume that the primary source of employment openings is the classified and display advertising in local and national newspapers. I can't count the number of times I have responded to an advertised position for which my background was a perfect match, only to not even get a card of acknowledgment from the firm. One of the executive recruiters I interviewed for this book told me two important things with respect to advertised positions. First, many of the best positions, particularly senior-level ones, aren't ever advertised, because the perception is that the best people don't bother to respond to advertised positions. Second, corporate personnel administrators usually have a list of keywords for each position.

**Bernie C. Jordan**
4297 Maple Street
Pittsburgh, PA 15201
(412) 555-0000

## Experience Summary

MAJOR MINICOMPUTERS CORPORATION (1987–Present)

*Product Manager, Database Systems (5/89–Present)*

Product manager for distributed DBMS development effort. Responsibilities include (1) gathering and validating customers' product requirements, (2) marketing the product to internal and external organizations, (3) coordinating pricing, packaging, and scheduling efforts with product and engineering teams, and (4) managing third-party contracted software development effort.

*Principal Software Engineer, Database Systems Tools (10/87–5/89)*

Responsible for analysis, design, and development of next-generation CASE database management system tools and utilities, as well as investigation and utilization of object-oriented software engineering methodologies and practices. Successfully developed two data modeling tool prototypes. Performed software system integration analysis tasks, including specifying interfaces with other CASE and life cycle support tools. Analyzed competitive CASE tools.

XYZ CONSULTING, INC. (10/86–9/87)

*Business Development Manager*

Responsible for business development, proposal generation, and hardware/software integration design. Program manager and chief software integration designer for multimillion dollar (>$6 million) PC-based office network for the U.S. Navy Finance Center (2500 users). Managed two multivendor Live Test Demonstrations, one of which included active participation by five firms and equipment/software from fifteen others. Prepared project pro forma cash flow, income, and balance sheet financial statements.

U.S. AIR FORCE, HEADQUARTERS STRATEGIC AIR COMMAND (1982–1986)

*Software Design Manager and Ada Prototype Developer (12/85–9/86)*

Managed a 10-member development team that designed and engineered a distributed air defense warning system featuring real-time sensor communications, color graphics displays at each workstation, a variety of user interfaces, and large-screen displays.

*Chief, Intelligence Systems Communications and Control Section, and Intelligence Communications Programmer (10/82–12/85)*

Responsible for designing, developing, and maintaining communications and systems software on one of SAC's major intelligence computer systems. While managing the six-member section, implemented nine new sensor circuits. Duties also included responding to emergencies at SAC HQ.

**Figure 9.1**   Sample résumé.

COMPUTER CONSULTING SYSTEMS, INC. (1982–Present)

*Managing Partner and Founder*

Provide microcomputer-based consulting, software, and seminar services to small business firms in Nebraska and Kansas. The three-partner firm, supplemented by subcontract programmers, specializes in database-based information systems for a variety of industries, from telephone communications firms to construction supply companies. Client support and supplemental consulting work continues to date utilizing subcontract assistance as necessary.

NEBRASKA STATE UNIVERSITY (7/82–5/89)

*Adjunct Professor*

Taught graduate classes in database management systems, computer consulting, and VAX/VMS.

NEW MEXICO STATE UNIVERSITY (1980–1982)

*Computer Center Consultant (5/82–10/82)*

Responsibilities included database management system evaluation, testing, and prototyping, consulting services for University administrative departments, and analyzing and correcting academic and research community programming problems.

*Research Assistant, Management Information Systems (6/81–5/82)*

Managed a 10-member programming staff in the implementation of an automated systems analysis/systems design programming set. The automated system was a portion of a continuing multiuniversity research effort into the capabilities and opportunities of computer-assisted information systems design, and was a forerunner of commercial CASE tools.

*Teaching Assistant/Instructor, Management Information Systems (8/80–8/81)*

Full-charge instructor for a variety of management information systems classes, including COBOL programming, data structures/database management systems, and information systems in society. Responsibilities included planning all lessons, assignments, and examinations, as well as grading all student work.

**Education Summary**

Master of Science, Management Information Systems, New Mexico State University, College of Business and Public Administration, 1982.    3.83 GPA.
Bachelor of Science, Computer Information Systems, Arizona State University, College of Business Administration, 1980.    3.54 GPA; graduated cum laude.
Numerous professional development and systems-specific training courses.

**Publications**

Article on real-time systems design, *Computerworld*, September 12, 1985.

**Figure 9.1**   *(Continued)*

| Languages | Systems | Technologies |
|-----------|---------|--------------|
| Ada | DEC VAX Family (VMS, Ultrix) | DBMS: SQL, 4GLs, |
| COBOL | UNIX workstations (Sun, Counterpoint) | and other query |
| FORTRAN | Sperry Univac 1100 series (Exec 8) | and programming |
| Jovial | DEC-10 (TOPS-10) | languages |
| Basic | CDC Cyber 175 (NOS/BE) | Object-oriented |
| Univac Assembler | MS-DOS microcomputers | technologies |
| C | Apple Macintosh microcomputers | Artificial intelligence |
| Pascal | DEC PDP 11/70 (RSTS/E) | and expert systems |
| Lisp | | CASE |
| | | Systems integration |
| | | and networks |

**Security Clearance**
DoD Secret

**Personal Interests**
Running, weight lifting, golf, horses, investment finance

**Salary History, References, and Personal Background Are Available Upon Request**

**Figure 9.1** (*Continued*)

If your résumé is missing that keyword, it is often automatically discarded even though you may be extremely highly qualified for that position. For example, if the magical keyword is "CASE tools" and your résumé notes experience with "data and process modeling tools" your résumé might be targeted toward the trash can *even though the two are really the same thing!*

Given this heartening bit of information, where do you find information about career opportunities? The primary source is usually through personal contacts, including friends of friends of barbers of friends of...well, you get the idea. This is extremely critical, especially if you are seeking to relocate. Even if people don't know of any openings in their own organizations, they may know of other organizations who are hiring.

Second, executive recruiters (headhunters) provide another source of openings. Particularly if you are planning to relocate, a national recruiting firm can be a valuable source of assistance with respect to the job search process. Be advised, though, that some recruiters are paid by the companies they represent, whereas others are paid by the job searchers themselves. Be certain to ascertain the payment policies upfront to avoid any nasty surprises later.

Job fairs are another source of employment contacts; they provide a way to conduct preliminary, screening interviews with a number of companies at a single location. Bill Marion, the Career Success Profile of Chap. 2, obtained his position with San Mateo County through a job fair. I've been to some job fairs that weren't the least bit productive and others that were a bastion of good contacts. In order to conduct a complete job search, though, job fairs should be part of your arsenal.

### Letters and résumés

All of the above searching options require a high-quality résumé (see the section on résumés in this chapter) as well as a cover letter, tailored to each situation and company, highlighting your strengths and abilities and why you are *the* person for the open position. When responding to newspaper advertisements, your letter should be the first weapon in your arsenal. There is no guarantee that the personnel people will read it, but the absence of a tailored cover letter may put you at a disadvantage and lump your résumé in with other hundreds or thousands.

### Follow-up phone calls

You should, when pursuing a particular opportunity, be very persistent in your follow-up phone calls. The key is to try to get past the personnel people to the manager or supervisor actually responsible for interviewing and hiring. There are a number of ways to find out who the decision maker is, including calling the organization's central number and asking for the manager of the department in which the opening is likely to be. With a bit of persistence, you can usually get through to the hiring manager and at least be able to supplement your résumé with a bit of personal selling. Some people feel awkward about this tactic and feel it may actually put them at a disadvantage by being perceived as too pushy, but if the position you are seeking is in sales, business development, or another area in which aggressiveness is a valued asset, your aggressive pursuit of the interview may turn out to be a factor in your favor.

### Interviewing

As with résumé writing and job searching, this section will briefly summarize the many factors of interviewing. The most important thing in your interviewing process is to be prepared. Learn as much as you can about the company and the organization with which you are interviewing. Think about answers to the questions you are likely to be asked with respect to your goals, strengths, and weaknesses (see the section Hiring Others). Know about the geographical area if the firm is located elsewhere than your current residence.

Don't bad-mouth your current or former employer. You don't need to sugarcoat every answer you give with respect to why you are leaving or why you left other companies in the past, but don't give answers like "They were a bunch of scum! And losers too!" Instead, be tactful. If you left because you didn't receive a raise and promotion despite many promises, say that "There were some financial and career commitments that were discussed at the time I joined the firm that weren't met. We tried but were unable to reach an understanding with respect to my contributions to the company." That sounds somewhat better to someone interviewing you than "They stiffed me on a raise, and didn't give me a promotion either!"

Be honest in your interviewing, as was recommended with respect to your résumé. Don't exaggerate or invent your accomplishments, and don't lie about any unfavorable information. You obviously shouldn't volunteer information that doesn't flatter your abilities and career, but you should have practiced, thoughtful answers to what you have *learned* from your failures in the past, how you never made the same mistake again, and so on.

Stress real accomplishments. If you have always completed software development assignments within the scheduled time, state that fact. If you were able to cut overhead in your department by 25 percent, stress that to the interviewer.

Show up promptly for the interview, and have an air of confidence—but not arrogance—about you. Try to convey that you *know* you are the best person for the position, and there is much that can benefit both you and the company after you are offered the position.

If at all possible, try to avoid salary discussions on the first interview. If pressed, avoid exact numbers; give ranges like "the mid-50s" or say, "I am looking at an overall compensation package, including base salary, incentive rewards, and other aspects. I don't necessarily have a magical salary number." When in doubt, try to give a slightly higher salary requirement than you would accept. Try to know what the applicable ranges are so you don't price yourself too low or too high.

Finally, ask to know the follow-up procedure. Will there be another interview cycle? Who will be contacting you, and in what time frame? Is there any other information you can provide?

The interview is the time when you can convince the hiring decision makers that you can do the work required. If, for example, the position is as a software developer in the electronic funds transfer (EFT) area of financial applications but you have no EFT background, this is where you can stress that your real-time missile warning systems background in the Air Force is really the perfect match for the EFT job. After all, you might convincingly state, both EFT and missile warning involve communications networks, real-time programming, high availability and failover, and other aspects common to both applications areas. From all the study you have done in the EFT area, you would then conclude, you are confident that your background gives you the perfect match for this position.

## Negotiating Employment

The rule to remember after receiving a job offer is that nearly all aspects are negotiable. That includes not only salary but benefits (to a degree), relocation, perks, date of starting a new job, amount of vacation time, and other job factors. If at all possible, try to remember that, once you have received a job offer, you are negotiating from a position of strength. The company wants you to join. If you feel the salary offer is inadequate, make a counteroffer and negotiate a mutually agreeable financial package. Request stock options; ask the company to cover the cost of relocating, including temporary living and house-hunting trips. Occasionally, you might be in a position of weakness, as when your spouse is relocating to a particular geographic area and this is the only job offer you have received from that area. The company doesn't have to know that; even in tough job markets, if you are valued enough for them to extend an employment offer to you, the odds are that you are valued enough that a fair, equitable employment package can be negotiated.

## Mentoring

The concept of mentoring is often misunderstood. Many people view it as nothing more than "kissing certain posterior anatomical portions of another person" (I need to be tactful here with my vernacular). In truth, mentoring is simply using the guidance, on a semiregular basis, of someone within your organization with knowledge and experience who can assist you in performing your duties as well as planning your career. It doesn't have to be your direct supervisor or manager, and in fact it's often better if it is someone who doesn't have direct line authority over you. If you are a junior software developer at a vendor, your mentor might be a product or marketing manager from an organization that you hope to join someday. He or she may be able to give you valuable advice on what accomplishments and rounding out of your background you need to reach your near-term career goals, as well as how to posture yourself for long-term career success.

How do you find a mentor? You don't walk up to someone and directly ask, "Will you be my mentor?" As soon as everyone else present is finished laughing hysterically, you're probably in for some massive be-hind-the-back derogatory references. It's better to have lunch in the company cafeteria with someone whom you think might be of some assistance to you and ease into the mentor relationship; basically, it's like building any other kind of social relationship. You may go to someone with a particular problem, or ask his or her advice on which college locally might be the best at which to pursue a master's degree.

In male-female mentor relationships, you need to be careful of im-proprieties. Even if there is nothing social or personal going on outside the business relationship, there is likely to be gossip among fellow em-ployees and others. Be careful not to jeopardize your career in the pro-cess of trying to help it.

## Hiring Others

Everyone has his or her favorite horror story about interviewing for a position. My personal favorite is when I was leaving the Air Force and considering a consulting position with a Big 8 (at the time; now it's the Big 6) accounting firm. I arranged an interview with one of the Big 8 in Phoenix, and was requested by the person coordinating the interview to bring a copy of my first book, *How to Be a Successful Computer Consultant,* with me. As the interview got under way, the manager of consulting operations for the firm asked to see the book. He thumbed through it, looked at me, scanned the book a bit more, looked at me again, and then asked, "Did you write this book yourself?"

I wasn't sure exactly from what angle his question was intended, so I answered, truthfully, that it was my work alone. We then proceeded a bit more with the interview, whereupon he interrupted the line of questions to once again ask if, indeed, this *truly* was my own work, and was I sure no one had collaborated with me. Resisting the extremely strong urge to sarcastically reply "No, my mommy helped me; I just drew the pictures," I tersely replied once again that the publisher did the cover art and the camera-ready copy, but the entire manuscript was written by me, only me, and *no one but me.* Needless to say, the rest of the interview was entirely unproductive, especially when 30 minutes into the process the other person abruptly rose from his chair, announced that it was golf time, and wished me luck as he left.

Most of you have had experiences similar to this one, especially in in-terviews for that first job after college. As your career progresses, es-pecially if you move into the supervisory and managerial ranks, you will find yourself on the other side of the interviewing table. We have discussed the interviewing skills needed when you are looking for a position; now let's look at the skills you'll need when you are the one making recommendations and possibly decisions as to whom to hire. Here are eight key questions to ask someone you are interviewing:[2]

1. *Why are you changing jobs?* Just as it was recommended that you don't speak too negatively of your current or past employer when you are interviewing for a position, neither should someone whom you are interviewing. Extremely negative remarks can be a warning sign of a perpetually disgruntled employee.

2. *What did you like best about your last job?* An interviewee should have a thoughtful, honest answer, especially in an area beyond the basic mechanics of a job.

3. *If you could have made improvements in your last job, what would they have been?* A candidate's creativity and his or her willingness to take a stand on important matters can be determined from the answer to this question.

4. *Who was the most interesting client you had in your last job, or what has been the most interesting job or project so far in your career?* More important than the actual answers are the reasons given, which can gauge whether or not the interviewee values challenges in his or her positions.

5. *Describe the best person who ever worked for you or with you.* An understanding of the candidate's values can be drawn from his or her answer.

6. *What kind of people annoy you the most?* Traits contrary to those possessed by the interviewee usually constitute the answer to this question, which in turn provides another part of the picture of the candidate.

7. *Describe emergencies in some of your jobs for which you had to reschedule your time.* As opposed to simply asking "Will you work extra hours when necessary?", this is a highly accurate gauge of the interviewee's priority system with respect to "after-hours work."

8. *In which way would you like our company to assist you if you join us?* A balance between wanting too much assistance and not wanting any help is the desirable answer. Someone who appears too dependent on the logistics of joining a firm may not be able to manage tough situations, whereas someone who is too independent may not feel any loyalty to the company and could leave in an unexpected manner.

There are a number of critical success factors in hiring quality people other than interviewing skills. References should be carefully checked to verify, as completely as possible, a candidate's academic, career, and other background. Any inconsistencies should be noted and reviewed with the job candidate. Be aware, though, that one or two minor inconsistencies do not automatically indicate that the candidate is taking liberties with the truth. Frequently, a job candidate might remember items that his or her busy supervisor may not recall. Major discrepancies, such as a candidate claiming a degree that turns out never to have been completed, should be a warning sign. There are cases of successful people who have faked degrees and had very productive and profitable careers, but for the most part the untruthfulness of a candidate in this type of matter could be a trouble spot ahead with respect to his or her job.

Job candidates like to be told the truth about their prospects for a particular position. As have I been, many of you have been strung along about a particular position only to never get a firm offer. Don't do that to others; if situations have changed since an interview and a slot is in question, tell the person when he or she calls or inquires. You may not want to lose that person, but it does more damage to your company's reputation in the job market to gain a reputation as a firm that doesn't have solid job openings. It's better to be as up-front as possible with respect to these types of positions; treat the candidates as you would like to be treated.

Finally, accept negotiations about salary and other job characteristics on the part of a prospective employee in the way you would if you were on the other side of the bargaining. If a candidate rejects a job offer on the basis of salary and you have some say in the salary offer, gauge whether or not the employee is worth an increased offer.

## Your Value System and Priorities

One of the persons I interviewed for the Career Success Profiles in this book, who shall remain anonymous with respect to this quote, told me, "I could be making a lot more money [working in another capacity]. But I make a good living, get to live where I want, and manage my business in a manner I feel is best."

Feel free to read ahead, because I plan on using this space to espouse my own particular ideas on the subject as I have done at several points earlier in this book. This is a very important concept to understand with respect to planning your career. I have alluded several times to matching your abilities, desires, and goals to the position and career path you wish to pursue. Most of us will never make it to the executive boardroom and the corner office on the 70th floor. That does *not* mean that those who do are the successful ones and the rest of us are less than successful. Each person's goals and objectives change over time, and although the corner office and the presidency of a corporation might be a goal at, say age 21, such other priorities as families, community involvement, and outside activities may affect your decision points in your career path in subsequent years.

Each career move you make should be balanced not only against the factors discussed in the first chapter and later throughout the book—technology, the economy, and the rest—but also against your value system and personal goals. For example, a high-salaried, executive position with fantastic perks and benefits that requires nearly full-time travel may not be compatible with your family and other goals. If you value things like Little League coaching, being home for family birthdays, and having time to go for long hikes in the forest, you need to judge *for yourself* if you are willing to make the sacrifices necessary for that position. *There is no crime in electing to have other things in your life aside from work.* It is true that, in some companies, the failure to devote yourself 100 percent to your work is not only career-limiting but potentially threatening to your employment stability. If at all possible, avoid that type of company and its culture unless you are willing to meet those norms (see Chap. 4). One of the nice things about the computer career field is that a number of positions and career paths can be pursued on a contract, part-time, or other than full-throttle basis, permitting you to have an active, successful career and still have time for other things.

The point is that there are no right and wrong perspectives on your career with respect to your life as a whole. Some people are happiest in their work environments; others view working in the computer field, or in any other profession, as a means to earn money with which to do other, more important things. You must assess your own values and objectives and use that insight to guide your career decision making as much as all of the other factors we've discussed in this book.

## Written and Verbal Communications Skills

One last topic to emphasize for this chapter—and this book—is the importance of communications skills to your career. I'm not referring to data communications and networks, though, as mentioned in the preceding chapter, that is one of the strongest areas of the computer industry. Rather, I'm referring to written and verbal communications skills.

I can unequivocally state that many people in the computer industry have extraordinarily poor written communications skills. I can't count the number of requirements documents, business plans, and specifications I have reviewed or received over the years that are full of syntactic and semantic errors and simply are not well written. Your career is often predicated on your ability to communicate, both on paper and verbally. At a minimum, throughout your career you will probably find yourself writing:

- Requirements analysis documents
- Specifications
- Feasibility studies
- Documentation, including internal documentation, user's guides, and reference manuals
- Requests for proposals (RFPs)
- Proposals, both solicited and unsolicited
- Business plans
- Product development support documents such as launch plans, marketing documents, customer support plans, field test plans, and other documents that are customarily part of the product development life cycle at major vendors
- Business letters

The ability to communicate clearly, concisely, and accurately is often critical to career success, particularly in the managerial ranks.

Verbal communications skills also are important. You must know how to tailor presentations to the type of audience you have, as well as how to effectively use slides, charts, and other visual aids.

If your verbal or written communications skills seem to be deficient, it would be highly advisable to take a course in technical or business writing or join an organization that helps polish presentation skills.

## Summary

This chapter briefly summarized a number of supplemental topics that are important to your career in the computer industry. Most of the topics can be researched more thoroughly through books and articles, on-the-job searching and interviews, and other sources. Though the chapter's topics were covered in a rather compact manner, this does not mean they are less important than the more fully explored subjects of the earlier chapters. Good career planning involves a number of variables, including the supplemental ones visited here.

## Career Success Profile: Stuart Sandler, Self-Employed Computer Consultant; Former Sales Manager, ComputerLand

### Education background

B.S., Management Information Systems and General Business, University of Arizona, 1983

Graduate work in MIS at the University of Arizona

### Career

IBM, 1980–1983, variety of positions

ComputerLand, Tucson, Arizona, 1983–1991

    1983–1985, Computer Specialist

    1985–1986, Assistant Manager

    1986–1988, Operations Manager

    1988–1991, Executive Account Division Marketing Manager, Commercial Accounts Division

Self-Employed Custom Software Developer and Consultant, 1983–1986, 1991–present

Stuart Sandler spent 8 years with ComputerLand in Tucson, Arizona, and he has seen both the boom and the bust in computer retail sales. During those 8 years he progressed through a number of increasingly responsible sales and sales management positions before leaving in early 1991 to reenter the consulting and software development world in which he moonlighted during his time at ComputerLand.

Stuart's career in the computer field began during his college undergraduate days in the early 1980s, when he worked at IBM through the University of Arizona's cooperative education program. He held a variety of positions at IBM in technical and planning capacities before entering the retail computer sales world following graduation. His work at ComputerLand included retail sales to individual customers as well as corporate and commercial accounts.

### Best career move

"Going into sales following graduation. Most of my classmates went to work for large MIS organizations; I wanted to stay in Tucson, and originally went into sales somewhat reluctantly. Given that 1983 was probably the height of the computer retail business, the position ended up being very beneficial from both the career and financial standpoints."

### What he would change

"I would have taken more advantage of the many training opportunities that were available. For example, Novell network training was available when I was at ComputerLand, but unfortunately I didn't attend that or other training sessions."

### Long-term career objective

"To be a chief information officer at a large company."

### Recommendations for others

**General.** "When in college, take advantage of the cooperative education program. Even if it takes you a bit longer to graduate, you may come out with two years or so of practical, real-world experience that will make you stand out from the others with whom you are competing. This is especially important in a tight job market like we have today.

"Be aware of trends in computing. 'Big iron' (mainframe systems) are going away in favor of distributed systems. Your career should be oriented towards integrating and developing distributed systems as opposed to learning mainframe-based, batch COBOL and FORTRAN environments and techniques.

"Always tell the truth, and always return your phone calls. These seem like two unrelated, insignificant items, but especially in the sales world they are both signs of customer *service*. The key for sales, and careers in general, is that customer service. Given the rise of end-user computer, the mystique of software development and other computer skills has gone away, and clients will no longer put up with insensitive, unsupportive computer professionals. To be successful in a competitive environment, customer service is often the differentiator.

"When things are no longer fun in what you are doing professionally, it is time to move on. Given the amount of time—40 hours per week, often much more—you should be doing something you enjoy. There are so many different jobs you can do in the 'computer field' that you should strive to find a job that matches your personal and professional objectives. Very often, your success is predicated on the ability to 'sell yourself' as *the* person able to perform some job function, and disillusionment with what you are doing will adversely affect your ability to do so.

"Keep talking to people. Develop your own network of customers, suppliers and vendors, and current and former coworkers. Paths often cross and recross in this industry—and business in general—and the more people you know the better off you will be."

**On sales.** "Computer retail sales are in a downslide, probably for good. Less and less dollars are available for retail stores. The chains are moving away from showroom floor selling and more towards corporate and commercial account sales. Operations are being consolidated, and there are far fewer opportunities in this segment than when I began in 1983.

"The trend is to be either a low margin, high volume dealer, or a value-added reseller (VAR)—someone who takes equipment and software and develops whole systems.

"If you want to get into computer retailing, don't. Seriously—if you really think that this is what you would like to do, move to a smaller town and work there. There may not be much money, but there are probably better opportunities than in major markets.

"You might also look at what I would consider the ultimate sales job: working for a vendor with dealers as your customer base. This way, you have a small, loyal customer base with fairly fixed, established prices. This is likely to be one of the few strong growth segments within computer sales. Note that it's from the vendor side, as opposed to retail, direct to the customer, sales.

"For anyone in sales, you should know as much as possible about your products. You should come across to your customers as a SE (systems engineer) who has been trained to sell rather than a professional salesperson who just happens to be selling computers this year instead of automobiles.

"You should also partner yourself into a group that has a high degree of synergy. If your specialty is database products, you should work closely with other salespeople who specialize in, for example, LAN and CASE products. In this way, you can sell solutions rather than point products.

"Know your market. Markets are very different geographically; some are very price-sensitive, while others are driven by quality—real or perceived. Depending on where you are selling, your sales strategies are likely to be radically different.

"You should also continually update your skills. Attend trade shows, vendor training, and whatever other training is available to keep you at the leading edge of both products and technology."

## End Notes

1. This section adapted from Alan R. Simon, *How to Be a Successful Computer Consultant,* 2d ed., McGraw-Hill, New York, 1990.
2. Robert Half International, *How to Hire Smart,* 2d ed., 1990. Some remarks and comments provided by this author.

# Index

## ABOUT THE AUTHOR

Alan R. Simon is managing partner of Simon & Associates,
a consulting and software development organization. He
is the author of *How to Be a Successful Computer
Consultant* (McGraw-Hill), now in its second edition.